THE ARDENT BIRDER

On the Craft of Birdwatching

Todd Newberry & Gene Holtan

TEN SPEED PRESS
Berkeley | Toronto

Publisher Phil Wood dedicates this book to Tom Cuthbertson,
his first author and source of many others
along with many years of friendship.

1🕊️

Ten Speed Press
Box 7123
Berkeley, California 94707
www.tenspeed.com

Distributed in Australia by Simon and Schuster Australia, in Canada
by Ten Speed Press Canada, in New Zealand by Southern Publishers
Group, in South Africa by Real Books, and in the United Kingdom
and Europe by Airlift Book Company.

Cover and text design by Nancy Austin

Library of Congress Cataloging-in-Publication Data
Newberry, Todd.
   The ardent birder : on the craft of birdwatching / Todd Newberry ;
illustrated by Gene Holtan.
      p. cm.
   Includes bibliographical references.
   ISBN-13: 978-1-58008-715-5
   ISBN-10: 1-58008-715-9
   1. Bird watching. I. Title.
   QL677.5.N47 2005
   598'.072'34--dc22
                                          200502090
Printed in the U.S.A.
First printing, 2005
1 2 3 4 5 6 7 8 9 10 — 09 08 07 06 05

FOR LOUISE

Life touches life.

Charles Hartshorne

CONTENTS 🪶

ACKNOWLEDGMENTS

It takes a village to raise a book, too. Some of my Santa Cruz, California, birding companions have vetted the text: early on they were Lois and Wally Goldfrank, William Park, Barry McLaughlin, and David Suddjian. Others include patient friends like Keyt Fischer, Kerstin Wasson, Ann Thiermann, Bruce Bowman, John Wilkes, and Irene Herrmann. I have passed the manuscript like a samizdat book among many other readers, too, who have helped me generously. Since a reader's hesitation signifies a writer's lapse, I have tried to adopt virtually all their suggestions or at least have rewritten the passages they flagged. Birders who have visited Santa Cruz from all over the country have also gone away—I should be embarrassed to reveal—burdened with a copy of my manuscript; many of them have offered insightful comments that I have incorporated.

A lot of what I have to say in *The Ardent Birder* has come my way from a lifetime of mentors. Bill Eblen introduced me to birding when I was lost in boarding school. Then I had the luck to fall in with some of the great midcentury birders of

Acknowledgments

New Jersey's Urner Ornithological Club: Al Eynon, Lee Edwards, and especially Floyd Wolfarth. They were patient and generous and immensely influential teachers.

I am indebted, as well, to the writer Lawrence Weschler, the historian John Dizikes, *Harper's Magazine* senior editor Luke Mitchell, and the legendary publisher Jack Shoemaker for encouraging me over several years as I tried to find this book's way eventually to press.

I have leaned very hard on my wife, Louise, and on my daughters, Ellen Newberry and Elizabeth Chapman, one a teacher of writing and the other an editor. They have been fonts of sound counsel about this project and also about everything else in life. They have borne my efforts with intelligence and grace, patience and affection.

In the summer of 2003, when *The Ardent Birder* seemed to be headed for the attic, Louise urged me to ask the artist Gene Holtan to illustrate it. He did more than that; he transformed it with extraordinary drawings. For me, the experience felt like having a composer put my libretto to music: what an exhilarating moment! Even its title seemed to take on an operatic lambency. *The Ardent Birder* became a conversation between its text and its drawings, one we invite its readers to join.

Louise died suddenly in the spring of 2004, in the second spring of her life, and so this project just about died, too. But a few months later I encountered my old student Tom Cuthbertson, of *Anybody's Bike Book* fame. In a deft move, I saddled him with the manuscript. He kindly took it to Ten Speed Press's owner, Phil Wood, who gave it the home that, in fact, Louise herself had long ago predicted would be its best, if ever we could find the door in. There, Lily Binns nurtured it into a book at last. We all read stories about the improbable ways by which idiosyncratic books roam toward their publication. They are true.

INTRODUCTION

The conversation usually goes like this: "Oh, you are a birdwatcher! Last week I saw the strangest bird . . ." I nod sagely: "Sounds like a Cedar Waxwing." A name named, we move on to weightier stuff. But what about my being a birdwatcher? What is *that* like? *The Ardent Birder* is about being a birdwatcher: who we are and what we do. In part, it is what I want to tell my inquirers, if only they would ask.

But I have written this book for active birders, too, for ardent novices and even what I call "the varsity." This book is an occasion to revel in some of our tribe's folkways, what a friend has called our "lovely madness." After all, birding—unlike, say, bridge—regularly throws accomplished veterans and rank novices together. In that mix, what is old hat for the varsity may well describe the very dilemma some nearby beginner is struggling with. In that spirit, dear reader, read on, if not for yourself, then for others.

The book's first essays describe "Our Day." Every field day we birders wrench ourselves at dawn from our bed's cozy embrace, go afield to snoop into other creatures' lives, savor our little triumphs of identification, and cope with birding's peculiar tribulations or celebrate its splendid moments. As weeks pass, our days become "Our Year." We come across rare birds or at least ones that are new to us; we get keener at our craft; we play daffy birding games; we go on birding trips far from home and host traveling birders ourselves. And just as we may reflect on our day at the end of it, so also, as winter comes on, we tend to take stock of the past year's accomplishments. That is when we buoy our spirits with vows like "wait'll next year!"

In mid-book I pause for "A Philosophical Interlude." Just by observing birds closely for a while, what can we learn about the processes behind nature's patterns? Out in the field, what kinds of questions (very few, it turns out) lead to answers that do not start with "maybe"? How can we meet that discomfiting challenge, "How do you know?" or, more searching still, "So what?" In some ways natural history is disarmingly accessible; it gives us nature stories. Yet for some naturalists (including me), it is the epitome of intellectual subtlety, "the queen of the sciences." The essays in this chapter ask why.

Good birding demands good habits. And so we will attend to some rather neglected "Skills": just standing still, stalking birds and luring them into view, pointing them out to others (without actually pointing), listening as carefully as we look, counting birds in flocks, even finding the bird at all by making your binoculars your friend, not your frustration. I leave to others the inculcation of tactics that mark crisp identifications. The skills I explore are more ones of mind-set, of approach, applicable, by the way, to a lot more than birding.

Birding's pricey "Gear"—so many toys! I address this subject with hesitation. Tools are not skills, nor should they be blamed for anyone's clumsiness. Binoculars and spotting scopes, especially, seduce and bankrupt. After a nod in their direction, I move along to more unlikely paraphernalia that also serve me well: monopods, camouflage, mirrors, even my bookmobile.

Finally, I take up a prospect that both tempts and daunts many birders: leading bird walks for the local club. I lead a lot of club field trips, for better or worse. Even if you never lead any yourself, eventually you may find yourself curious about the dynamics that attend them, rich as they are in companions as well as (let's hope) in birds.

To me, companionship in birding is vital. When I started watching birds some sixty years ago, John Kieran had just written in *Footnotes on Nature*, "It probably is true that a man sees more things and makes more searching observations in the field when he is alone, but there is a virtue in companionship that makes up for any decrease in the supply of clinical notes. A pleasure shared is a pleasure doubled." The pleasure of birdwatching is what *The Ardent Birder* is most about.

WHO WE ARE

We ardent birders share not only a skill and craft but also a state of mind—more, a state of heart, one akin to love. All the usual explanations of why such an improbable pastime as birdwatching should be so profoundly rewarding—the thrill of the chase, days of companionship outdoors, enigmatic identifications solved, competition and even scorekeeping, witnessing nature in action, times and places of great beauty—all these sorts of reasons fall short unless they acknowledge those extraordinary moments when, as Charles Hartshorne once put it, "Life touches life." Honoring these moments, I think, is the largely unspoken bond among ardent birders. When we do talk about why we go birding, time and again these private experiences are what we birders recall as "when lightning struck."

For the psychologist and philosopher William James, our only sure knowledge is subjective: beliefs as thoroughgoing as they are mysteriously arrived at. We are never entirely confident of what our intellect lets us know, even if it does steer the rocket to the moon. When life touches life, our heart responds, whatever sense our head, looking on, makes of the occasion. And so I would venture that birding, for all its skill and paraphernalia, is at base an emotional enterprise. While we work at our craft, what sustains us are intense attachments to nature, nourished by our encounters. Those of us who feel these stirrings of the heart really are what the epithet calls us: *ardent* birders.

Most of us have fallen casually into birding. I started as a boy in boarding school when William Eblen, a teacher there, took me along to a nearby reservoir one April day to look at migrating ducks. I had thought all ducks were park-pond Mallards, but here were pintails and wigeons and strange geese, even blue ones, feeding close by; and there we were alone with them that cold afternoon. A month later I was startled to see a flock of goldfinches and Indigo Buntings—all gold and ink—flitting through the bushes outside the chemistry lab. One night that spring, a roiling mass of Chimney Swifts poured through the open flue of the library's stately hearth and careened about the reading room seeking places to roost. Thrashing brooms did no good: we had to grab the birds in our bare hands and fling them by the hundreds back into the darkness. I still remember holding them—their still, soft weight. One morning that May a tree by the pond was festooned with warblers—unheard-of little creatures that I alone observed. Everywhere that spring, birds seemed to be bearers of astonishment. While my head absorbed classroom lessons, my heart was seduced, bird by bird. Another dawn a meadowlark catapulted into the air almost at my feet. That put me over the edge. By that summer, I was an ardent birder.

We birdwatchers vary in our skills. Most broadly and vaguely, of course, we call ourselves beginners, intermediate, or advanced (what I call "varsity") birders. We all serve our time as beginners, as I did back there in boarding school and for a couple of years after that. But just as most of us workaday folk put ourselves in the middle class, so also most of us who have been birders awhile see ourselves as intermediate ones. Some of us, with practice and experience, while still intermediate in many ways, do gain some advanced skills; we join birding's varsity. We varsity birders can be proud of how

*Like musicians, we birders gain
our skills by practicing them.*

far we have come, as we sort out perplexing gulls and sparrows. But now and then we realize afresh that we are still part of birding's middle class, because now and then we are stumped. Faced with strange birds, we tend to grope.

Beyond even the varsity lie birding's major leagues: the professionals and those rare amateurs who are as good as the pros. The gulf is great: the distance in skills between birding's varsity and its major leagues resembles that between the varsity and the major leagues in baseball. But we needn't be discouraged; what the major leaguers are to our varsity eyes, we are to beginners. Dazzle is relative.

Beginner, intermediate, varsity, major leaguer. Here is an analogy: A beginner identifying an unfamiliar bird shuffles through its traits as though they were a mental handful of loose flash cards arranged almost haphazardly—brown, duck-like, streaked, big . . . We have all been through this clumsy exercise. As we gain intermediate and even varsity facility, we riffle the cards with Rolodex speed and orderliness. Separating out confusing species may slow us down, but getting that far feels automatic as we sort through the traits, and so the choices, toward an ID: Clark's Grebe or Western? Greater Scaup or Lesser? Which female teal? Mourning Warbler or MacGillivray's? Which juvenile sparrow? Major-league birders negotiate these same traits and choices, but they do so in the lightning way one handles the vocabulary and grammar of a familiar language. In a word, major leaguers bird fluently.

Many top birders have exceptional eyesight, uncanny hearing, and a powerful visual memory, like an accomplished musician's aural recall of the repertoire. But while the muses may dispense genius, we learn our skills ourselves. The virtuoso birder and musician alike have *achieved* their skills by giving them a singular priority in their lives. For most of us, birding is an avocation. That is why most of us, despite our ardor, are still intermediate birders (or for that matter intermediate musicians).

That said, we do have skills aplenty. We get our binoculars on the birds—even if sometimes clumsily. We quickly identify familiar species, and we know when we have met up with an unfamiliar bird—because then we proceed, well, more slowly. Our bird guides stay pocketed—except when we are perplexed.

Multitrait comparisons enrich our identifications—even if we forget at first to look at the very trait that matters most. Many bird families come easily to us—even if a few, such as vireos and sparrows, resist our efforts. Days afield no longer frustrate us as they once did—despite certain moments. In sum, we feel the pleasure of competence, even though "intermediate" keeps asserting itself.

We varsity birders know our local birds very well. We can identify almost all our local songbirds all year long by both their songs and their calls. We know our fall warblers and winter sparrows and can figure out almost all the local gulls confidently (if not always accurately). We are puzzled by only a few birds during a long day afield. But then we really are puzzled. Then we do sense our limits, and for a while we bird on thin ice even in our usual haunts.

Trips to distant birding hot spots, especially, pack our varsity lists but try our skills—or even, if the trip goes on too long, our spirits. Faraway birds are all very well, but it can be a relief to get back home. Now our Rolodex fairly hums again. Once again the oddities spice our day but don't overwhelm it. In our own bailiwicks, the rarities we come upon may test us, but they seem manageable, if only by their very rarity. Given home field advantage, we bird well, and so with pleasure. More than that, familiar species and surroundings invite us to move beyond the question "What is it?" to "What is it doing? What is going on?" That is, as the ornithologist Byron Butler has put it, we move beyond birding to *watching* birds, beyond sightseeing to observing, to being investigative reporters of nature. Then, while the birds we watch aren't the first of their kind we have ever seen, the things we watch them doing may be.

Among the ardent, birding never wears out. There was plenty that enchanted me as a beginner, but skills that come simply with focus, practice, and experience now lend a certain subtlety, I think, to the pleasure I get from each birding day. The fact is, the varsity really does have more fun.

The day starts.

OUR DAY

THE DAY STARTS

Ardent birders arise in darkness. I pack my gear into a tote bag the evening before so I am not left looking for binoculars, scope, tools, books, license, and keys at the last moment. Gremlins thrive in the dark, and they like to spend pre-birding nights hiding precisely these things. Knowing I have beaten them lets me sleep.

Sleep, yes, but fitfully. No matter how early I usually get up, something about rising even earlier to go birding afflicts my sleep the whole night before. After midnight, my insomniac brain keeps calculating how many half hours there are between, say, 1:45 and 4:15. Can I still trust my alarm clock this time despite its loyal years? Could I turn it off without realizing it—have I already? Now I have an hour left, but have I gotten any sleep at all? Can I risk a little more? And anyway, why do I have to get up so early? Do the birds care?

Now comes the hardest part of any birder's day: actually getting out of bed. There, it's done—do not backslide now!—and a few steps put comfort at a safe distance. The worst is over. But did I turn off the alarm? And did I set a second one that

Why get up so early? Do the birds care?

will go off like a fire bell after I leave the bedroom? Ah! There are my slippers; already the day is improving.

I get up very early because that leaves plenty of time—an hour at least—to get started. Breakfast sets the whole day's pace. While I munch my toast and nurse my coffee and make my plans, I try to frame one or two big questions to ask in the course of the day ahead. Questions we can answer in the field take their own time forming, like darkroom prints developing. Maybe I will take on the challenge again of identifying young gulls. Or I will stop and really watch ravens "at play" and ask myself how I draw that inference. Or I may decide to focus on a pattern of distribution: how do gulls in mixed flocks sort themselves by species? This reflection lets me venture forth with nurtured questions, not rushed ones. Rushed questions are usually as inadequate as rushed coffee.

Time now to pack some lunch; sure enough, I almost forgot. Then I step into a waning night. Toward the east the sky has lightened; dawn's goddess is stirring from her couch. I head out into a magical world.

SNOOPING

Let's admit it: what birders do is spy and snoop. We stare at birds as they eat and fight. We watch them at their domestic chores, as they raise their young, as they cope with awful moments. When a bird meets its worst fate, we raise our binoculars and watch. We watch birds in their most intimate moments, too: preening, defecating, sleeping. We do not avert our gaze from birds at courtship or even at sex. Our snooping is plain enough to people who see us at it, and it causes the occasional shrugged shoulders or smiles. I think it arouses from time to time a certain shyness in the birdwatcher, caught out like Actaeon watching Artemis at her bath.

Today's question: How do gulls sort themselves out?

Fortunately birds seem to go about their lives despite our watching, yet I am sure they are affected when our binoculars' giant eyes turn their way. At the least, they look back at us. On the birders' Web forum BirdChat, Byron Butler has noted how much birdwatching involves birders and birds looking at each other. Visual creatures like birds and people often seem to share a deep-seated disquiet upon being blatantly stared at, especially if it includes being pointed at. As birders, anything we can do to soften our stare or mask our pointing probably lets us snoop better.

We can empathize with scrutinized birds when we catch other birders scrutinizing us. Birders along the seashore or in marshes do this, for example, when, rather than make a long walk for nothing, they try to guess from afar by our behavior what we are watching. And we have all noticed distant birders trying to recognize us through their binoculars. That's exactly what we are doing with our birds.

A deep-seated disquiet upon being stared at.

Where people live or work, snooping can lead to what I call "visual trespassing." We stand in the road, but we may train our sights, for example, on feeders that hang close to houses or even next to windows; or we may look at bushes near us that are directly in line with windows farther away, so that, even if inadvertently, we appear to be watching the windows, not the bushes. Most people don't like optics-laden strangers inexplicably studying their windows, eyeing the family at breakfast. Who wants the morning's first question to be "Why are all those people out there staring at us?" In our culture, unsolicited stares tend to threaten and offend, even when they are inadvertent. When in doubt, I simply ask the residents if I can look at their birds. They almost always let me, and with relief that I am not casing the place. When they refuse, I figure that they really do have something to hide, and so I go snoop elsewhere.

TRESPASSING

We birders must snoop; that is in the nature of our craft. But trespassing: what a dilemma! In Great Britain some countryside boundaries do not apply in full force to hikers. That access took years of debate and acts of Parliament to bring about. Here in America fear of strangers is wide and deep and getting worse. As John Stilgoe has commented, we are wary of people who scrutinize the ordinary. It takes only moments to ask if we can enter someone's yard or farm or if we can examine it closely from the road. If access is granted, when I'm done I leave my name and a list of what I found there; I

I leave a list of what I found.

may even add a note that I would like to come back, thanks very much. That list often pleasantly surprises my hosts.

If the situation feels awkward, I bird somewhere else. The foreclosed acreage may tantalize, but skipping it probably won't much diminish the day's birding. If it does—for example, if that spread has the region's only marsh—discreet persistence may produce occasional access eventually. That won't come by trespassing.

If I do succeed in getting some kind of regular access to a birdy place, I like to turn my thanks into more than words. For example, I can give the host a field guide. I keep a couple of good-as-new copies in my car to give away as thanks for such welcomes. And I try to stick to agreed-upon routes. Especially on a farm, what may appear to be an innocuous detour may land you in fields you should never have trampled or among creatures you never should have met. But do try to meet the dogs. And even if it is not at the moment an especially birdy place, come back soon and often enough, letting the owners know each time, so they can get used to your visits before the big day when great birds do show up.

A few landowners hesitate to let birders on their place because they have heard tales of what can follow upon the discovery of rare birds: crowds of chasers, cars everywhere, cattle frightened, gates left open, crops trampled, dogs in a terrible state, even litter, and general disarray and fury. When access is iffy, we can announce a private place's rarities, if we do so at all, as found "on private property" and leave it at that. This is not being selfish; discretion protects limited access that may grow some day to include others. If the bird is literally outlandish (that stint at the sewage ponds, that wagtail in the gated resort) consult with the owner: can you escort friends to see the bird? If the answer is no, work up your record well, because you are going to be that bird's sole observer there.

Landowners also worry that natural marvels, once known, spell trouble. What about that heron rookery in the copse, that seasonal pond, that riparian stretch, that (good Lord!) grouse lek? Why not bar access and so thwart discovery? I have no answer to paranoia, but maybe birding the place now and then with the owner, admiring and sharing its pleasures, can allay the worst suspicions. Maybe the welcome has been guarded, but I seek only an entrée, not an embrace. We can encourage eventual warmth (or at least an amused toleration) by our care when on the place, by our discretion in reporting what we have found there—and by leaving our thanks, a bird list, and a field guide.

EXPECTATIONS

When I was a kid, I was sure a thousand kinds of birds lived in New Jersey. Soon enough I found out that only a few hundred had ever been recorded in the state, but by then (a fretful youth) I also had taken to heart the adage that anything with wings can turn up anywhere it can fly. Well, yes and no. Yes, the more our skills grow, the more we ought to take a wide range of possible species into account when identifying a perplexing bird (or for that matter when ID'ing any bird at all). But no, riffling mentally through the flycatchers of Brazil merely distracts from the effort of identifying the local *Empidonax*, and gulls of distant ports scarcely need complicate most days at the local dump. Outlandish birds are literally that: a Xantus's Hummingbird in Canada's Vancouver? a Brambling in California's Santa Cruz? a Swallow-tailed Gull in Monterey? a Eurasian Kestrel on Cape Cod? These strangers are thoroughly exotic, which is why they cause bird records committees so much writhing about their origins. We bird with more modest expectations.

And yet, and yet . . . someone must be the first to see these interlopers when they show up. If discovery falls to you, you must recognize a rarity as such, even if you are baffled by its kind. Consider just gulls. Recently a top local birder here beside Monterey Bay found and described what was almost surely a young Band-tailed Gull, far from its home on the Andean coast. And then it was gone, a one sight wonder. A Swallow-tailed Gull from the Galapagos once spent a few June days on the Monterey Peninsula, then left, never to be seen again. Ivory Gulls have turned up in Tennessee and southern California, Ross's Gulls on Long Island and in Delaware. Outlandish! Maybe gulls of distant ports merit our study after all. But errant shorebirds do, too. And so do wandering songsters. One needs to know all the local, expected species and all their plumages well. Then the unexpected species at least grabs attention, come what may of the scrutiny and the frantic phone calls that follow. Being ready for extraordinary encounters is part of the reward for learning the familiar birds so well. Of course, another reward for that effort is to know the familiar birds so well anyway, even without rarities intruding.

Field guides have little bird distribution maps, and beginning birders (or the rest of us far from home) tend to consult them perhaps too closely. Where should a map draw the limit around a species' local movements and its wider wanderings? What is the geography of expectations? Or the *ecology* of expectations? For the most part, bird species stick to characteristic habitats, even to particular vegetation structures. No meadowlarks in the forest, sure, but which warblers flit high in the treetops and which low in the bushes? All those sparrows, but which species among them are most likely on a beach and which in a swamp? Those perplexing flycatchers: which species prefers what part of the forest canopy? Those four species of wintering longspurs, so difficult to identify in winter or even to find, tend to sort themselves out by subtleties of ground cover. We bird not just in places but in *kinds* of places. When we find vagrants and other rarities far from their usual haunts, they are at least in their usual *kinds* of haunts. A report of a suspected species that is out of place both geographically and ecologically is fair game for, well, suspicion. A look around at the scenery may bring us up short; the species we are wondering about should not be lurking in a place like this.

But there are downsides to expectations. For example, we can dismiss too quickly some visiting birder's report of a rare bird, or even our own sightings. Jack Connor writes in *The Complete Birder* that he was so surprised once to see ravens in southern New Jersey that he forced himself to call them crows, only to find out later from others that they *were* ravens. Here in California I once decided, after troubled scrutiny, that I was looking at a weirdly plumaged Black Tern, for surely it could not have been that extraordinary rarity from Europe, a White-winged Tern. Luckily, the bird stayed around and sharper birders later realized it was indeed a White-winged Tern. Connor warns beginners against too easily expecting the unexpected, but he suggests that intermediate birders try to "unexpect the expected," and so make every familiar species prove itself. We can do this only by *really looking at every bird* until we are truly satisfied with our identification. The major leaguers do this fast; the rest of us have to take our time. This habitual care will mostly confirm the birds we ordinarily encounter; but now and then, and more often than passing glimpses can, care will reveal rarities, recognized for what they are. Then, even if tentatively, accept the implausible. Tell others so they can set you straight—or share your discovery! To err on the side of the angels is still to err, as I learned once again with that tern.

At its worst, expecting only the expected encourages that old birding slogan, "It must be a . . ." We all do this now and then, as when we whiz by roadside fence birds. I call this bad habit "glance-and-go." When I feel it creeping on, I take a break or change my pace or go to a different habitat that may restore the birding juices—anything to get myself back to really looking and listening. If that doesn't do the trick, maybe it's a good day for yard work.

Even so, sometimes I find myself identifying familiar birds carefully enough but then hurrying on, almost bored. This is the time to avoid glance-and-go by cultivating what Proust called "seeing with new eyes." John Dewey, in *Art as Experience*, describes the effect of this new sight as one of moving from recognition to perception, a nice distinction in birding. Here are some ways to make this move:

- Notice and enumerate *aloud* a bird's diagnostic, bird-guide traits.

- Notice trait by trait how it differs from, say, two similar species.

- Notice something about the bird that you have never noticed before. You can do this again and again. Quick sketches will direct your eye.

- Sort its plumage into feather groups, from lores to vent to tip of tail, from wing base to wing tip. *Call them out.* Examine each of the bird's unfeathered structures, too. The second half of David Sibley's *Birding Basics* is a superb guide to these features.

- Watch the bird's behavior when you see it actually do something, and describe *out loud or in notes* what it does.

- Take in both the bird and its surroundings until it is no longer just a name on a list but rather part of your encounter with its world.

When flagging stamina and creeping ennui settle on a day afield, and on some days they are bound to, stratagems like these work wonders by revealing wonders.

Notice something about the bird
you have never noticed before.

MEETING OTHER BIRDERS IN THE FIELD

I shamelessly try to imitate the ways of the best birders, hoping thereby to gain their skills. A few major leaguers I have known are aloof, but most of them are wonderfully helpful and cordial. Recently I was on a group tour with a famous guide in a famous birding hot spot. He spent what seemed like a couple of hours each day greeting and chatting with other birders. When we discovered especially good birds, he chased after other birders to show them, too. We found all the species we sought, some of them very rare. And we found, as well, friendly fellow searchers. I came home even more resolved than before to greet other birders in the field and to do so with more than just a smile. We are one clan. Surely we can manage at least a trailside pause to say

*Meeting other birders
in the field.*

hello. Few days afield are so jammed that they cannot absorb some affability.

Of course, not even my gregarious guide could hail all the birders that swarm over Big Bend or Plum Island or converge on Point Pelee or High Island in the high season. But most places, most days, we birders don't come in swarms or even hordes; in fact, over most of the continent we rarely come across one another at all. When we do, we are bound to encounter various levels of skill. In some pastimes, disparate skills create awkward social situations. For example, for fear of being asked (or seen?) to play beneath them, tennis whizzes and bridge demons are notoriously leery of the enthusiastic beginners who may lurk around the court or the card table. But better birders hardly risk having to play a match with the tyros they meet on the trail. Can an hour or two searching the woods together, if it comes to that, really hurt? And anyway, that shy fellow with the funny hat may be a very fine birder indeed.

Trading names and news cannot ruin the day, and it may *make* the day. Even so, sometimes an odd standoffishness hovers. My greeting falters. Gimlet eyes appraise my binoculars. Why do I feel inspected? This is not paranoia at work; my wife, Louise, has watched it happen. She calls this kind of encounter between birders "dogs sniffing." And what if, hand extended, you stumble onto a birding god? Act your usual self. Real gods tend to be splendid; would-be gods vex but amuse. Savor *both* sorts of divine encounters.

RAIN

This ought to be a proverb: "It never rains on real birders." Actually, from time to time it does rain (or even snow), maybe even steadily, but usually a lot less in the field than how it looks through a window. Shrewd glances at the sky along with a feel for the local weather patterns can find dry holes in many wet days. In the mountains, for example, the clouds may part over valleys while storms march along the ridges. One cannot see these spectacular skies through the roof of a house.

In *The World of an Insect*, Rémy Chauvin remarks that most days of "steady" rain are actually ones of roving showers with only drizzle, if even that, in between. Separate veils of rain sweep the countryside. On these days the most intimate lay of the land affects how much rain reaches the ground: lots of it on hillocks and less in the miniature rain shadows of the hollows. Cans put out over a hilly pasture will hold surprisingly different amounts of rainwater at the end of most wet days.

Songbirding in the rain usually results in a glum morning. But those hours can be redeemed by coffee and cake beforehand and more of the same after calling it quits. In *Listen, the Red-Eyed Vireo*, Milton White recounts his very first bird walk, a wet one on an early spring morning in Ohio. The improbable Olney Bird Watchers, oblivious to the rain that day or any other, trudged through a winter-blasted landscape on the edge of town. At last they came upon their morning's only bird, a robin singing and gathering wet string for its nest. To their delight, it even took some that they offered. Inspired, they trooped off to build a brush pile for sparrows, while in the distance the robin "had begun to sing again." White's little book will cheer up any damp birder.

When it rains we have to choose what we chase— famously ducks, but also, if the season is right, gulls and shorebirds, which tough it out calmly on the flats and fields. A rainy day is a good time to devote a couple of hours to these birds. In open country during a windless drizzle, umbrellas make surprisingly comfortable refuges for spotting scopes, and gazebos and other such structures—usually nicely deserted in the rain—can shelter a lake-watch or a sea-watch even in a windy downpour. So can a cleverly parked car. The sea always seems ready to spring a grand surprise for any birder willing to venture out along the shore in a storm. The car or some overhang out of the wind becomes a cozy den, from which a spotting scope pierces beyond the surf. It feels as if the stage is set and the rain is a parting curtain.

From time to time it does rain.

The most ordinary birds often seem wonderfully strange in the rain.

In low latitudes and desert country, rain tends to fall sporadically as thunderstorms or as fast-moving weather fronts. Some New England storms and the winter rains along the Pacific coast can seem interminable; but they, too, have their erratic ways. It may scarcely comfort the wet searcher, but rain's mosaic behavior should encourage everyone to go birding anyway. The birds themselves, after all, are out there.

NO FLY ZONES

Why do No Fly Zones (NFZs) seem to afflict us intermediate or even varsity birders more than they do the major leaguers? In part because major leaguers hear birds that we missed. They pick up their faint noises, and so they know they are there. And they see more. They notice the slight movements of skulkers, and they decipher from afar the little shapes of perched birds. Jack Connor says, "They see more because they miss less." They build encounters where we miss the clues to them. Perhaps out of sheer confidence, major leaguers tend to be patient, both with clues and with the birds that must have left them. They wait and they listen and they watch.

Sometimes I practice the major leaguers' skill of *noticing*—which is what it comes to—by finding a few quiet birds in an NFZ, and then focusing doggedly on the slight clues to their presence. In the woods I focus on tiny feet moving the duff, a bending twig, the sound of leaves being gleaned, a fleeting shadow in the foliage, a shape that isn't a leaf, a quiet pip, an alarmed insect. This is detection in reverse. My goal is not to find a bird from its clues, since I already know it is there. Rather, it is to observe the bird in the very act of leaving clues. On another quiet day, I will have only those clues to alert me, and from them I will realize that a bird is there.

At least in woodsy habitats, an NFZ is rarely bird-free; the birds are sitting silently on the nest, sheltering from wind, cowering from an accipiter, or taking their siestas. On a quiet midsummer morning, stopping awhile and *listening* will reveal the presence of birds all around, hidden by luxuriant foliage, occasionally making little noises that are apparent only to someone who is *standing still*. But sometimes, especially in the open, a place seems to qualify as truly bird-free. On this tide all the mudflat's shorebirds have left to feed farther up the estuary; the ducks are nowhere on the lake; the little flock of wintering sparrows has abandoned its usual hedge. One has the sense of being at the dance hall after the dance. Other habitats beckon, and so I make my escape. A little later, a little farther along, birdlife seems miraculously to have resumed, like a world reborn. But of course, it has resumed back where I was, too; birds have returned there, or they were just pausing when I would not.

Birds were just pausing.

CRUMMY HABITATS

I have birded in many lovely places. But when I started, in northeastern New Jersey, I learned, as well, to scour landfills and look behind marshland factories and work over what I have since learned were toxic dumps. My mentors taught me that birds are where you find them. Vagrant birds, especially, may not be as picky about their surroundings as the birders who search for them. So now I include a few crummy habitats in my regular rounds. I don't mean shabby city street corners, but rather habitats like these:

- Farm ponds with weedy or cow-trodden borders
- Pocket parks
- Cemeteries of all sorts, especially their edges
- Big trash heaps and little dumps that have forlorn bushes
- Rural sewage ponds or other filthy wet places
- Landscaped highway flanks and—even better—rest stops
- Ugly hedgerows alongside farm fields and ballparks
- Abandoned, overgrown construction sites
- The shrubbier edges of parking lots
- Plantings at the busy entrances to tranquil places
- Vacant lots with unhealthy trees and brush piles
- Scrubby back beaches, especially if wet
- Seedy public picnic spots

Crummy places all, where nature cowers.

Mostly, of course, one searches these habitats in vain, but it doesn't take long. And once in a great while, patience will turn up a prize. This quick and opportunistic birding falls under the rubric "You can't win if you don't play."

Crummy birding places include public picnic spots.

WHAT MADE IT A DAY?

Another potential proverb: "It doesn't take much to make a birder's day." The tales we carry home often strike the patient listener there as modest. One day I finally saw how the neck of a Double-crested Cormorant droops half heron-like in flight while that of a Brandt's Cormorant is arrow-straight. That made my day. Another day on a glaring beach a teeny Snowy Plover chick watched me from between its tiny mother's legs. Once a Calliope Hummingbird inspected my hat. One winter afternoon I shared a dune with a Snowy Owl. These little incidents don't match spectacles like million-shearwater flocks, raptors' stupendous aerial shows, and encounters with great rarities; but they are no less day-makers.

Over many years of birding, I have rarely spent a day afield that did not provide some memorable impression: an unusual species, a familiar one in remarkable numbers, some bird's extraordinary behavior or its striking appearance, a close encounter, a play of light, a lay of the land, a question posed well, an idea nicely shared, an experience of "seeing with new eyes." I don't think I am particularly prone to these episodes. Rather, it seems to me, field days almost always reward birders with occasions that exceed expectations. Birding puts us in nature with such a wide sweep and yet such a precise focus that it invites peculiarly intense moments. They are so thorough, they feel to me like *plunges*: plunges into nature.

Sometimes the occasion is so surpassing, so breathtaking, so superb, we turn to one another and declare in exhilaration, "An Audubon Moment!" Other occasions come into their own when, the field day done, I go back over it mentally, and it takes lasting shape in retrospect. I keep a log with a few brief notes entered at the end of every birding day. What made it a special day? The log began in fits and starts, but now I attend to it regularly so that, years later, it will bring these hours back to life.

Some occasions feel like plunges into nature.

OUR YEAR

LIFERS, BVDS, AND RIES

American birders intent on their life or state or county
or annual or God knows what other list are dubbed, appro-
priately, "listers." In Great Britain they are called, with
Monty Pythonesque flair, "twitchers." In California, where
I live, I could keep fifty-eight annual county lists, and some
of my friends do that. Annual lists are a prescription for
perennial anxiety; and county lists seem to me to fence the
avifauna into political fiefs, the way surveying turns the land
into property. Keeping bioregional lists would make more
sense if we could agree on boundaries of that sort: watershed
lists or mountain range ones or coastal ones, say.

After much hemming and hawing, I now keep three life
lists: one of the species I have seen around Monterey Bay (my
bioregion), another of the birds I have seen in my now-home
state of California, and a list of all the species I have seen in
all of North America. Between the three I twitch enough to
satisfy, if that is the way to put it. Of course, as my North
American life list grows, additions to it ("lifers") get less

frequent; my Monterey Bay list has to provide most of my twitchy thrills, lifers only of the most local sort.

Meanwhile, when it comes to twitching all-American lifers, faraway places and exotic habitats and their birds beckon ever more seductively: South Florida! West Texas! Arizona! The Far North! And since we are talking about North America, what about Mexico? Very rarely, strange birds arrive on my home turf from some of these places, and I chase after them to lengthen all three of my lists at once—bioregional, state, and even continental—without traveling far at all.

I used to limit myself to an hour's drive to seek for myself a life bird that someone else had already found and reported—in birding jargon, a "staked" bird. Now I find myself going farther than that and regretting that in the past I did not deign (or more to the point, bother) to drive many more miles to see extraordinary rarities. Those Bristle-thighed Curlews and that Greater Sand Plover "a little too far" up the coast! That Little Curlew just across Monterey Bay! That Brambling that wintered right here in town when I was away. How could I have let these chances go by?

A life bird usually gets plenty of scrutiny. But sometimes the sighting is so unsatisfactory that it qualifies as a BVD: a Better View Desired. I wish I knew who invented this superb birding acronym; despite pointing fingers, it wasn't me. Better View Desired is the name of a valuable website that reviews birding optics. The name fits, as well, that flash of wing or silhouette that is enough, but only barely enough, to recognize a lifer. My first Northern Saw-whet Owl was mostly a shadow that flitted across the snow while I was somehow caught head down under some low cedar branches. My first Zone-tailed Hawk was a watery-eyed speck aloft; my first Painted Bunting was a winter female; for thirty years my only Northern Goshawk was a speeding blur in a deep northern forest. BVDs all.

Better view desired.

BVDs set the stage for RIEs: Radically Improved Encounters. My encounter with that Saw-whet Owl was an easy enough one to improve radically merely by looking up, as I did a few weeks later. My second Zone-tailed Hawk, only a week after the first, left the vulture flock it had been soaring with, floated closer and closer, and, to my astonishment, landed in a huge field in front of me. I was thrilled by my first sight of a gaudy male Painted Bunting years after I first saw the plain female—a lifer by gender, I suppose. Last summer, I strayed foolishly close to a nest and ducked as a Northern Goshawk dashed screaming into a tree forty feet away and dared me to approach. Definitely an RIE, and I escaped unscathed. But my only Sharp-tailed Grouse is still an airborne assumption, and the Tropical Parula remains for me a breast in dense foliage. I yearn for RIEs.

And then there are birds I saw so long ago that to see them again would be to see them in a far richer context of acquaintance than I had back then. More than that, my life list seems to be in peculiar flux, shrinking at one end as it grows at the other. Species from my boyhood fade from memory, even as I add new ones now. I think there should be a rule: we should have to remember clearly at least some encounter—not necessarily the first, but at least *one*—with every species on our life list. Under this rule a lot of lists would shorten! A lot of old sightings would decay into BVDs. While some RIEs would radically improve any acquaintance at all with the bird, others would feel like reunions, perhaps with the disconcerting emotions those occasions may entail.

But of course birding is much more than adding to lists. Experience teaches that when we birders turn away quickly from birds that we "have seen before," we miss plenty. The most familiar species hold surprises for us: traits we have never noticed, behavior we have never seen, a setting that refreshes our sense of harmony with the natural world

A Radically Improved Encounter.

around us, a reunion with our own past. It pays to honor every bird we encounter.

ON BEING DOUBTED

It happens to us all, and it always stings. We report some rarity, but even our friends doubt us. And then worse, a bird records committee rejects our report on grounds of proba-ble misidentification. We have been dismissed by a committee of people who never saw the bird! They believe their pals, not us. Visitors to a birding hot spot are particularly likely to suffer this ignominy at the hands of the locals when they call in reports to the Rare Bird Alert. Dammit, why bother?

Whether Alexander Pope, in his "Essay on Criticism," was thinking of records committee members or of a reporting birder, I leave to you:

> Of all the causes which conspire to blind
> Man's erring judgment, and misguide the mind,
> What the weak head with strongest bias rules,
> Is pride, the never-failing vice of fools.
> . . .
> Pride, where wit fails, steps in to our defence,
> And fills up all the mighty void of sense.

In *Down and Dirty Birding*, Joey Slinger put the matter this way: "When they used to burn witches, the burnee's last gasp often was 'Compared to turning in a rare bird report, this is a day at the beach.'"

Now grill yourself:

- How well did you see the bird? What equipment did you use?

- What is your evidence? *Notes*, including sketches, *taken on the spot*, are essential. For reports of exceptionally rare birds, records committees insist increasingly on photos, too. Uh-oh, no pix? Time to buy more pricey gear.

- From all you observed and noted, exactly what suite of traits—one trait is never enough—convinces you of your identification?

When the birds records committee doubts your report . . .

🐦 How familiar are you with this species (and with this sex and age of it)? When did you last see it? Did you use a field guide to make this call? To confirm it?

🐦 Is this species "unmistakable"? Male Painted Bunting, Wild Turkey, adult Bald Eagle, Greater Roadrunner, and remarkably few other species may be "unmistakable." The legendary Ludlow Griscom insisted none at all were.

🐦 If the species is not unmistakable, what common species might it remotely be confused with, maybe because of an aberrant plumage or a structural abnormality? By what means and how thoroughly did you eliminate that alternative as you *actually observed* your bird?

Rarity that it is, is there another rare or even rarer species it could possibly be? Instead of a Marbled Murrelet, could it be a Long-billed Murrelet? Not a Little Stint but rather a Red-necked Stint? Not Xantus's Murrelet but Craveri's? Not an Arctic Warbler but a Dusky? Did that alternative occur to you while you were observing the bird? What traits (again plural) ruled out the alternative? Gulls are especially treacherous in this regard, roaming as they do.

Is there the slightest chance that "believing is seeing"? Could the light or the particular view you had of the bird have played tricks and misled you, and from then on you were just buttressing your hunch?

What traits would have ruled out your ID? Did you look expressly for them?

Did the bird's behavior figure in your ID? Describe everything it did.

Do the bird's general and intimate habitats both make sense for that species?

Does the date make sense for the species you claim? Does its plumage (by sex, age, molt) make sense for that date?

In the past have you been confident of an exciting ID that you began to doubt once you were challenged? (Of course you have; we all have.) How have you improved your birding and reporting skills since then?

*How well did
you see the bird?*

🪶 Do you wish you could go back and check that bird? Of course you do! But precisely why?

🪶 Whom else have you alerted to look at your bird? With what result?

🪶 Would you accept at face value another capable birder's claim of this bird based on your notes? Do you understand exactly why you are being doubted?

Tough questions. And this last one raises the delicate converse of the painful situation you are in: knowing how it feels to be doubted, from now on you will doubt others diplomatically and sensitively.

When all is said, if you know you found what you claim but no one else believes you, then record it for yourself, put the episode behind you, and carry on. Your evidence—so often, there's no photo!—does not suffice to convince a committee even if it convinces you, you who saw and studied the bird itself. That Eskimo Curlew on Martha's Vineyard? That Little Stint in Salinas? That Grace's Warbler in Santa Cruz? Asterisks on one's personal records are just the thing for these records. Even the very best birders among us have a few of them, avifaunal orphans, each one a *rara avis* beyond any private doubt, every one of them treasured in our hearts. Think of the asterisk as a bright star.

But permit me a cautionary confession here. One afternoon long ago, while monitoring the fall hawk migration over the Watchung Mountains of New Jersey, I was sure I spied a flock of thirty Sandhill Cranes flying south very, very high. Unmistakable! I was alone, the excitement faded, and something made me, a shy teenager then, keep this extraordinary record to myself. Many years later I saw the same sight. They were Snow Geese. Maybe you saw Snow Geese, too.

STUDY DAYS

No matter what our skills, we all need study days, when we put aside the chase and hunker down alone to study birds' particular traits, including detailed clues to identifications. I have taken to spending about one entire field day this way each month. For me these days are among the most tranquil and soul-satisfying.

One can amply *study* only three or four species in a day. In the field, studying means giving an hour's patient attention to one species, observing it over and over, honing eye and ear, focusing on its appearance, its behavior, its surroundings, drawing, and writing notes. The same species may well come under renewed scrutiny as the seasons progress—dabbling ducks in eclipse, gulls and terns as their plumage wears, sandpipers of different ages as they migrate through, spring warblers versus fall warblers, young sparrows versus adults. Study days have also helped me realize that molts, which I once thought of as just a seasonal challenge, confront me all year long—a whole new natural spectacle to follow.

By selecting beforehand the few species that will be my targets on a study day, I can read ahead in Bent's magnificent *Life Histories of North American Birds* or in the millennial, multi-volume *Birds of North America*, as well as in various field guides and handbooks. If ducks or gulls or shorebirds figure among my birds for the day, European guides, too, provide abundant commentary on widespread species. This preparation ensures that once I am in the field, I will study a bird I really know something about, rather than just some plumage with a name.

"Will you listen to that!"

A study-day habit that I learned early on and have cultivated ever since is to say a bird's name from time to time *aloud*, loud enough for me to actually hear, not just imagine. I say the bird's name aloud whenever I listen to its songs or calls, and I say it aloud the first time I see a bird I am going to study. And on study days I describe its traits aloud while I scrutinize them. So when I am at my lessons I mumble a lot. Sometimes what I hear myself saying tells me I am listening to an unfamiliar call or song: "Will you listen to that! Much burrier than usual!" or "It's like a slurred . . ." or "So why isn't it a . . . ?" When I am birding alone, talking to myself helps me make the bird the center of my focus. This eccentric habit carries the bird beyond being a passing object of attention; it arrests the bad habit of glance-and-go. By talking to myself, I am teaching myself, and, as teachers do, I stumble upon unexpected lessons and exclaim accordingly. If people are around, they may glance over from time to time, drawing their own conclusions.

Forcing oneself to study traits in detail cuts through the rush to identify a bird by its general impression, its so-called "jizz." ID'ing birds too often by jizz flirts with saying, "It must be a . . ." It can provide a false sense of fluency. Jizz, powerful as it is, emerges from specifics, no matter how fast we sort through them to reach it. So, to the extent that I can, I examine each structure, each feather group, each behavioral detail. As I force myself to pay attention to these specifics one by one, I am bound to discern details that I otherwise would have missed, and so I deepen my acquaintance with each species I study. This deliberate pace cultivates the habit of careful and orderly scrutiny. Then, when I next encounter an unfamiliar bird—so often an all too brief episode—this habit seems to come into play all the more quickly and, I hope, effectively.

In *Playing the Piano for Pleasure*, Charles Cooke advocates the "broken bones" method of practicing. When learning a piece of music, he says, do not spend your time replaying it all, fun though that may be. Rather, isolate and focus on and practice the parts that gave you initial trouble; then put the fragments back together. In this way, what was once weakest will grow especially strong, like broken bones healing well. In the same way, we can turn our birding weaknesses into strengths on study days. Even dowitchers and empids will perplex us less if we give them their due.

SCORECARDS

I am not competitive, but I sure as hell like to beat anybody who is. Even if most birders insist they are uncompetitive, birding does lend itself to, well, a certain rivalry. For evidence of this, consider birders' lists: monthly, annual, life, county, state, continental, global, idiosyncratic. Check out the record-keeping computer programs birders lavish attention on. Peruse the American Birding Association's (ABA) intricate annual compendium of bird lists. Read in its newsletter that this birder or that has reached a magic number; read its rules of listing and the debates that swirl about them. Listen to the cries of delight and alarm when the American Ornithologists' Union periodically revises the "official" North American bird taxonomy, with splits and lumps that raise and lower a lister's bottom line. There is even a World Series of Birding. If all this isn't competitive, why are so many of us keeping score?

To taste the competition, watch us listers as we list, us twitchers as we twitch. Watch us as we converge on great rarities. Listen to our tales of woe and, yes, even envy. For an ardent birder, fate can seem so capricious. The more skillful birders do see more birds; practice does pay off. But like a goblin, crazy chance keeps intruding. The sheer good luck of this bird flying over or that one jumping up makes our day.

Meanwhile, a rarity emerges from hiding only as all the birders depart. What a crapshoot!

Even amid this competition, the Big Day is special. Big Days are twenty-four-hour marathons to find the most birds ever in a city or state or some other region or to strive for some other extraordinary mark. Teams of a few varsity or major-league birders come up with staggering totals, occasionally exceeding two hundred species. A successful Big Day demands keen tactical planning, and it can pose strange ethical dilemmas, too. I recall some from the 1950s that Ed Stearns raised when a few of us in New Jersey's Urner Ornithological Club prepared for Big Days. Here are three:

- You have staked a Barn Owl nest in a rural shed. In the small hours of the morning, you peer into the shed and hear rustlings in the rafters. Perhaps, tantalizingly, a Barn Owl feather flutters down. But you cannot see the owl itself, and it doesn't call; the owl (for surely that is what's up there . . . it's not a rat?) just moves about noisily in the rafters. Can you count it?

- You visit a Long-eared Owl's nest before dawn for the day's only good chance to find this bird. You shine a flashlight up into the tree; there's the nest, but all you can see is the tip of the bird's—some bird's—tail. Can you count it? You hoot, and the bird looks down over the rim of its nest. You can see its eye glow in the flashlight's beam, but nothing more. Can you count the bird now?

- You find a Ruffed Grouse's nest, but for some reason— too noisy an approach?—not the parents. But there are a few just-hatched chicks. The clock is running, so you can't wait around. Can you count the chicks as "young grouse"? Replay the scenario, this time with only eggs in the nest. Can you count them as grouse in "extremely juvenile plumage"?

In the 1950s there was no ABA to keep us in line. Today, the ABA acts rather like birding's version of golf's USGA with all its rules. We have come a long way from simpler days, even if Ed Stearns's quandaries still beguile us. Golfers can play as they please when they play on their own, and we birders can count as we please on our own. Everyone's golf score is a personal one, and so is everyone's bird list. The game of birding, like the game of golf, is a personal contest and, when it goes well, a largely spiritual celebration. But when the competition goes public, we can thank God—I think—for the USGA and ABA.

Big Days are an extreme sport. One of my birding companions has come up with saner alternatives, such as a Big Weekend or even a Big Week. More dawns, more habitats, another chance—these are blessings instead of the Big Day's awful now-or-neverness. Or at least it feels that way until dusk on Sunday or on the Big Week's seventh day! But avoid a Big Month, my friend warns, because it can settle in like a thirty-day obsession. (I won't begin to comment on the obsession that ripens during those ultimate twitching treks, Big Years.)

I myself tend to favor still another game. Some mornings I try to find as many species as I can along a set route, as if I were playing a round of golf against par. I tend to do it alone,

Keeping a list.

but any number can play. I live next to Monterey Bay, California. My favorite local birding route for this game, as it hugs the Santa Cruz city limits, combines the open ocean and coastal reefs and bluffs, beaches and scrub, a large arboretum and a landscaped park, several riparian ravines, marshy ponds and a big duck pond, an abandoned farm and a new one, immense hillside pastures, some redwood forest, a college campus, and a very birdy sky overhead. It is a heavenly circuit. I give myself four hours to cover it, which sets a fast pace. Sometimes I rearrange the route's sequence, like rearranging a golf course's holes, and I may skip a habitat. But I don't add to the whole course anymore; that much is set. In birding as in golf, par is a goal to shoot for, not an average. My winter goal—my four-hour winter par for the course— is a whopping one hundred species . . . by lunch!

Not every birding locale is as rich as this one; some are even birdier. And of course par varies with the season, in many other places much more than it does here. The tempo of the day, though, is the same anywhere: species cascading in at first, then a too-long search for one bird or some other tactical error, an expected target or two missed, catch-up birding by clues grabbed on the run, the clock ticking and the map running out, the pressure mounting . . .

Two team competitions that a varsity Michigan birder has told me about also vary (and bring sanity to) the Big Day. These pit roads against roads. One is the One Mile Challenge, the other the One Road Challenge. In the former, a birder or a one-car team chooses a single mile of any road; in the latter, the entire stretch of any road inside one county qualifies if it keeps the same name. During the contest's morning, birders or teams can count any bird seen or heard from the road or from within, say, ten yards of it. But now for the heartbreaker: after each match the winning mile or road is retired from competition—not forever, I hope!

Still another craziness is the Big Sit. The rules proliferate, as rules do, but the idea is for a team to record as many species as it can in a day from within a seventeen-foot-diameter circle. Many years ago a group of varsity birders sat on a shrewdly positioned flatbed truck in central California's Elkhorn Slough and recorded 117 species in one day. That effort has barely been topped; I think a superb hot spot in southern California holds the current Big Sit record of 122. Since, as Tip O'Neill said of politics, all birding is local, so also are realistic goals; thus they vary enormously according to a Big Sit's season and place. Reaching them, even if they are modest numbers, can challenge the best of us. A hot spot's hundred species? A farm's forty? A city park's twenty-five?

A wintry tundra's ten? And of course, choosing where to put that little circle can test our wits even more than birding from it. No wonder the Big Sit is catching on.

These games are not everyone's idea of fun, not by a long shot. But if you thrive on competition, even just alone against par, there are field days for that. I admit I like them, uncompetitive though I am.

A PATCH OF ONE'S OWN

A mile up the road from where I live is one of the University of California's arboretums, a spectacular site overlooking Monterey Bay. Thirty years ago, when a macadamia bush and some eucalyptus trees were planted to start this arboretum, these fifty acres were just one corner of a huge upland pasture, with mucky wallows and almost impenetrable thickets where, as I recall, big and scary cattle lurked. Now most of the acreage has become gardens, copses, and horticultural workshops filled with expatriate plants from South Africa, Australia, and New Zealand. It is a nightmare for devotees of native plants but a splendid habitat for native birds. In the course of the year, a birder here will find close to eighty kinds of birds.

Beyond one arboretum fence line, a few slopes are still remnant ranch land; even now, cattle occasionally graze there. A creek has sunk gentle hollows across these pastures. Misbegotten attempts long ago to turn part of the creek bed into a reservoir have left two dikes. During the winter rains one of them holds back enough water to make a respectable pond amid the willows, and the other dike stops enough to flood a woodsy marsh. By late spring the water has seeped away into the caverns that riddle this land. But these bucolic surroundings are about to change. The creek and its hollows are slated for "restoration," which means the loss of some old attractions for wildlife—let's hope with the gain of some new ones. And along another fence line, the university plans to border this idyllic place with a big project: townhouses for people and cats.

As these acres have gone from pasture to gardens, their birdlife has completely changed, and more changes are in store. As the university campus intrudes, the pipits and

Monitoring a patch.

meadowlarks will leave the fields where they winter now, and tree-loving accipiters and Red-shouldered Hawks will replace the harriers and Golden Eagles and Red-tails that scour the grasslands. Quail flourish in the arboretum. When the new townhouses' escapee cats find those quail—and the thrashers, too, and the towhees and the other ground-loving birds that have adopted the arboretum's gardens as their own—they will think they have arrived in Heaven and the birds will learn about Hell.

I wish I had had the patience and the gumption to monitor this arboretum's birdlife over these past decades, for it has been like the stage of an ecological theater transformed while the play goes on. Do the arithmetic: had I visited the place for only a couple of hours weekly on the way to work, instead of just driving by, by now I would have documented some *three thousand hours* of ecological observations. What an opportunity squandered! And with all this activity afoot now around the arboretum's edges, who will record what next happens to the birds that live here? Someone should, anyone can—even I.

Monitoring a patch, even a glorious one like this arboretum, usually seems trivial as you do it. Week by week, not much happens, and what does mark the calendar as species arrive and depart is roughly predictable. The same date rolls around again, and mostly the same kinds and numbers of birds always seem to be there. Censuses go along briskly enough; but as the weeks stretch on, they can feel tedious. The data sheets fill slowly. Truancy tempts. That's when we need to remember the childhood hymn about how little drops of water and little grains of sand make the mighty ocean and the fruitful land. Here on our patch, those drops and grains are what we are monitoring. Over years, but imperceptibly day by day, life has transformed the place, just as the hymn promises.

Few patches are as fine as the U.C. Santa Cruz arboretum. But down the street from me developers have prettified an old quarry with a pond and some trees. Now it's just the four-acre habitat for someone to check twice a week. Around the corner is a city park—playground, lawn, trimmed trees, and a big duck pond—that, despite its unpromising look, has hosted dozens of species over the years, even rarities like a Tufted Duck. Elsewhere in town, a half-forgotten hillside cemetery catches the morning light and flocks of migrants. Places like these invite visits now and then; all the more reason to go there habitually and keep count.

Over whole seasons, most patches are birdier than they may first appear to be. A manicured riverbank park in another town never saw birders until a friend of mine began to walk through it regularly on his way to the office. In the decades since, he has found well over a hundred species there and all manner of changes in their populations. That river seems to be a little migratory highway. Sometimes the surprises can be embarrassing. One August afternoon forty years ago on the Big Sur coast, my wife and I followed a lazy river from the highway to the sea. It was hot and still; the path seemed all but birdless. "Well, Louise," I declared after an hour, "we can write off *this* place." "This place" has since become the Big Sur Ornithological Lab, one of the liveliest birding sites on the central California coast. Moral: In an unfamiliar place, be more patient than I was that day.

Counting birds is usually a cinch (but see "Counting Swiftly," page 148). You do not have to walk around like an inspector, data sheet at the ready. Work out a standard route, and then relax and bird. At the end of the tour, make a species list and put in the numbers as you recall them. You will soon fall into an accurate enough routine, despite some individual birds missed and others counted twice. On a patch, simple ways work.

Unlike the Big Sur Lab, most patches won't make ornithological headlines. Perhaps, like data-filled tributaries, the accumulating records of birds' comings and goings, of how their populations wax and wane, may combine someday into more ambitious efforts to understand a region's ecology. But what if they don't? What if your records gather dust? It doesn't matter. The very exercise of monitoring a habitat's ongoing birdlife instills some of a naturalist's skills, keenness, and patience. In fact, the sheer pleasure of following the seasons on a patch of one's own is reward enough. Take good notes!

FAR FROM HOME, OUT OF ONE'S DEPTH

The major leaguers can handle whole continents with (apparent) aplomb, but "home field advantage" has all too much meaning for the rest of us birders. The farther we go from home, the shakier we get. Every unfamiliar bird feels like a rarity; and if there is no local checklist, we are not even sure what *would* be a rarity. We suspect our identifications of even familiar species when they appear in new surroundings and among the unfamiliar birds there. Bird sounds, especially, confound. And sparrows! Despite all we have studied, when we are far from home so many of them are such puzzles. Nor need we be all that far from home geographically, if we are far from it ecologically: if we are used to lush surroundings, then in arid lands, say; or if we are inlanders, then when we are beside the sea or even on it; or if we are flatlanders, then when we venture into the mountains.

One reason we can feel all too far from home is that we can no longer trust our expectations. (About those, see page 18.) At home, we know which species ought to be around. IDs have that satisfying click of an expectation met. But in another province our confidence may be porous, and so also our identifications. The upside of this predicament is that, far from home and out of our depth, we tend to look more closely at everything we see, listen more acutely to everything we hear. The downside is that we may find ourselves muttering, "It's an X . . . Sure it is . . . Well, I think so." Welcome back to the throes of beginning birding.

Just a few days, especially with companions, usually suffice to bring our visual skills up to speed—not to home field standards but to a level better than the confusion that may at first hobble us when we go birding in unfamiliar places. Aural skills tend to lag behind, but they catch up, too, call by call. Optimism rightly prevails within a continent. Crossing the sea even within the middle latitudes is another matter; I find the gardens of Italy, for example, filled with baffling songs. And surely most of us have found that our first days in the deep tropics, birding or not, are overwhelming as well as exhilarating.

Traveling birders can—must—use bird-finding books. Once there were only Olin Pettingill's two guides for all of North America! Now dozens of guides and lists cover states, parks and reserves, metropolitan areas, and famous hot spots. We can consult ABA "Lane" guides and other books, and local bird club projects, the varsity birders' labors of love.

The ardent birder far from home.

We can buy them from the ABA, Audubon Society chapters (such as the society's bookstores in Massachusetts or Los Angeles or Tucson), dealers who advertise in birders' magazines and on the Internet, national parks, and some wildlife reserves. Many magazines publish short accounts of hot spots, too; for example, check the back issues of the ABA's newsletter, *Winging It*. Ask bird clubs wherever you plan to go whether they have written up their bailiwicks or at least compiled lists of the species there.

My shelves now groan with this kind of literature. I buy guides well before departure and carry them around to read bit by bit, to kindle my expectations or at least anticipations. Often I tailor (that is, cut up and rebind with staples and heavy paper) the where-to-bird guides. That way, I take along only the pages of maps and directions and bird lists I will need, not Baedekers to a whole state if I am visiting only one place there. By the time I go on the trip, I know the better-known routes almost by heart. And in the course of all this preparation, what pleasure I get from their names: Boot Canyon! Doodletown Road! Raccoon Ridge! Panoche Valley! Fort Jefferson! Sabal Palms! . . .

Far from home, help often comes most easily and pleasantly from locals. The *ABA Membership Directory* is a godsend for finding good local birders. Also, bird clubs with websites often list their trip leaders, who are probably ardent birders. The ABA directory now lists most of the country's bird clubs, too, and inquiries with them will turn up their most active members. As of 2005, many varsity birders have joined the online resource Birding Pal (www.birdingpal.org), which helps travelers find locals all over the world. Rare Bird Alerts and email groups provide still more names of active birders. By one or several of these means, we can put ourselves in locals' hands, as they would put themselves in ours.

Another ally far from home is a professional guide. Guides are not cheap, but neither is going to some faraway place and floundering alone. Many friends who have turned to them report superb days with pro guides who are friendly people and usually terrific birders. They include local varsity birders who charge to show visitors around, major leaguers who prefer not to roam with group tours, and tour guides taking on extra duties. Locals who charge nowadays usually put a "$" code next to their names in the ABA directory. But beware, they may not; to avoid an awkward misunderstanding, be sure to ask when you start to set plans. Many guides advertise in birding magazines and in newsletters like the ABA's *Winging It*. By now so many birders have used so many guides that word of mouth in particularly active bird clubs or on online birding chat groups seems the best way to check them out.

Besides setting forth on our own or with a personal guide's help, we have a wonderful alternative: organized birding tours. They are expensive, but for a single birder they may not cost much more than going on one's own if that includes staying in motels and possibly hiring a guide now and then. The best tour guides have precious information about finding room and board in isolated places and about especially birdy, often obscure roads and stopping places; and so they save the traveling birder all sorts of logistical woes. On a good tour one can just bird, usually with fine companions. The top tour organizers and tour guides have wide reputations, so here again active birders and their circles can be helpful sources of recommendations, including cautions about unduly luxurious or pricey groups.

Many birders go on tours to add species to their lists, others to see new ecosystems. I do it for both reasons, and I go on them, as well, because I have found them to be workshops with major leaguers. These leaders cultivate high-caliber identification skills and observational deftness. They have taught me new ways to get on birds at all, how to sustain birding acuity and be "tournament tough," how to play Dr. Watson to a leader who is usually an ornithological Sherlock Holmes, and how to be an investigative reporter of birds. I think good tour leaders can transform the way the rest of us look for birds and what we do when we find them.

But no guide or tour leader can replace preparation *before* a trip. We birders have to study and learn not only the identifying traits of what we may encounter, but also, before each trip, the distributions of bird species. We need to know where our own familiar birds roam (lest we assume they live where they don't, or that they don't live where they do) and which unfamiliar ones will greet us where we are going. Almost always when I make wildly mistaken far-from-home calls, it is because I am inadequately prepared for what birds live there. I am birding with old expectations, truly out-of-place ones, because I have not steeped myself in the new ones I need. It is too late to prepare one's expectations when one is already far from home; that is like packing after a trip has begun.

Fully four kinds of distributions—hence, expectations—apply to each species that we may encounter in a new place. The most obvious one is geographic: how likely is such-and-such a species to occur there at all? Those little marginal maps in the bird books will not suffice. They depict only the roughest of approximations, while our identifications make the most specific of claims. Unfortunately for the casual birder, really learning geographic distributions forces us to consult tomes: the American Ornithologist Union's weighty *Check List of North American Birds* and its periodic updates and the multi-volume millennial *Birds of North America*. But the exercise lifts us to a new level of acquaintance; these are varsity calisthenics.

A second level of distribution applies within species to subspecies; compared to home, a familiar species' "other" races may have unfamiliar plumages. Across their immensely varied ranges, for instance, Savannah Sparrows and Song Sparrows come in a great array of appearances. Even when they pose no problem at first glance, with more careful scrutiny I find myself muttering, "No, wait a minute, there's something the matter. . ." And songs and calls can be disconcertingly different. To me, the Spotted Towhees that live in southeast Arizona sing almost like coastal California's Bewick's Wrens, and Bewick's Wrens along the lower Rio Grande sing like nothing else I have heard. Soon enough we get used to these new guises; but until then, our days afield can include some bizarre miscalls and many false alerts, most of them avoidable with earnest preparation.

Still another distribution is seasonal. Breeding, wintering, migrating: how likely is a species to be *where* we are birding *when* we are birding there? Locally published resources can help crucially on this score, especially if they include monthly bar-graphs or other such data. (For much of the year, whole-season statements like "common in winter" can be as treacherous temporally as those little maps are spatially.) Again, the best resources of all are the locals if they know the rhythms of the region's birds.

A fourth distribution, as I mentioned in "Expectations," is by habitat, often on quite a small scale. Juniper and Oak Titmice earn their names by the trees they prefer. Pelagic Cormorants tend to perch apart from Brandt's. Wintering gulls do not all hang out simply "on the beach." Forest birds do not live vaguely just "in the trees." And forests themselves often show complex, three-dimensional patterns. We know this well enough at home, but we can forget (or not notice) ecological patterns when we are disoriented in our travels and thrown into whole new ecosystems; so we come to birding grief where the plants of strange deserts or foreign woods "all look the same." Our expectations should make ecological as well as geographical sense.

We know our local birds' four kinds of distributions almost in our bones. But far from home, we need to bird with new eyes and ears, and only patient study beforehand and keen attentiveness in our new surroundings will let us do that. Even then, when I bird far from home, I find myself

It can be a relief to get back home.

continually questioning and re-affirming what I have learned for the occasion. Day by day, encounter by encounter, as I get more and more to declare, "Yes, it is!" about some tentative identification or perplexed observation, my confidence returns. Eventually I may trust what I think I see and hear. Preparation hastens that day.

After a couple of recent guided group tours far from home, I have stayed on in the area for several days to bird on my own or with locals. This has turned out to be an unbeatable combination: a tour with all its lessons and the regional acquaintance it provides, and then further birding independently. By the time I have set out on my own or with a local companion, I have put behind me the indecisiveness that first daunted me in the new landscape. My post-tour birding nails down the previous days' new skills and brings new confidence. At last, I feel like a competent birder again. My solo flights during these post-tour days have always left me feeling fulfilled and matured as a birder.

Still, I cannot deny that, for all we may learn in new habitats and distant places, and as exhilarating as our field days there can be, it can be a relief to get back home, where nature, even if flatter, may seem to fit more comfortably, like our very own slippers.

LOCALS

Even when you are not very far from home, the counsel and especially the company of a skillful local birder can make a huge difference. The where-to-bird guidebooks seldom direct a visitor to the exact stretch of stream, the particular vista, the pool in the marsh, or the fence in the pasture that the locals go to as a matter of course. And for a hard-to-find species, the locals probably have a favorite place to try. While guidebooks understandably slight places with ambiguous access, the locals know whom to call, how to behave, and how to bird those places. In "Far from Home, Out of One's Depth" I mention the ABA membership list, Birding Pal online, and clubs as travelers' sources of local names. But what do you do if *you* are the local that some visitor seeks out? How do you make the most of the opportunity for both of you? And, visitor or local, how can you match skills if you do not care to escort a beginner or you blunder upon a birding god?

First, let's play the host. When an inquiry reaches me from afar, in my reply I ask for a list of "target species." Of course, this puts a listing flavor on the prospective day. If you don't like that, you need to tell your inquirer so, because in my experience most visitors do want to see particular species, which is why they inquire in the first place. Whether or not we actually get together to bird, that list of target species usually speaks volumes.

It immediately lets me know how familiar the visitor is with my area's birds. Can the visitor find almost all the target birds alone, or would a companion make a big difference on that score? If someone asks me about a single species, I reply with directions; often, if it is easy to find, that's that. But a list of a dozen target species (or sometimes two or three dozen!) suggests the need for some teamwork.

Sometimes I just annotate the proffered list and maybe offer my company, and I don't hear any more except thanks and perhaps a trip report. But more often than not, the ensuing correspondence—email was made for this!—leads to teaming up, and with a clear mission.

If we decide to join forces, the target list lets me plan an itinerary, big or small, half a day or a full day or even more than a day. It lets me envision route and pace, duration, and almost hourly goals. And it frequently brings to mind other locals who might join us to make up, as the maître d' says, a "party of four."

Finally, an inquirer may decline to send a target list: "Oh, I have no special birds in mind, just a day enjoying your scenery." Or "I'm just beginning, any birds are fine." Hmm.

If you prefer, you might simply wish such inquirers well, maybe with recommended vista points; you have already been very helpful. But inquiring beginners are very rare indeed; at least, what beginner except a truly ardent one would go to the trouble of seeking out a local? And as for more experienced birders, if they just want to see the place, their interest in the scenery leaves me free to choose the haunts I love most. I have spent superb days birding around Monterey Bay with exactly such visitors. They are often fine birders, just not twitchers.

Now let's play the visitor. You choose a name from the ABA directory or the Birding Pal website and send an inquiry. Your hosts are almost bound to be good birders. Who else would flag themselves as local resources? If the reply suggests that your birding styles differ a lot, you can leave it diplomatically at that, with thanks for the info, and go back to your resources for another name. Of course, some great romances probably have started in such a mismatched way.

Matching skills does pose uncertainties. If that matters to you, here is a parallel and a proposal: Just as traveling birders may seek local ones for a day afield, traveling amateur musicians may seek fellow players for a night of Beethoven or Brahms. An inquiry implies from the start, "Let's play." But what if you are an excellent cellist and find yourself with a beginning pianist? For half a century now, a group called the Amateur Chamber Music Players (ACMP) has helped its members avoid this mishap. Its members take a self-graded test of their competence as musicians. And so the names in the ACMP directory have grades, and intelligible ones because everyone has taken the same test: A, B, C, and some "amateur" pros. (The ACMP insists that no musician ardent enough to join it rates a D.) Think of the awful nights that have never happened! Think of the great nights that have!

Birding is not like playing string quartets; veering out of ornithological tune scarcely matters as it does with Schubert. But matching skills and intensity does help make for a happy day of birding as much as a good evening of playing music. True enough, some of our kind do seem to puff themselves up in birding as much as in music and lord it over the rest of us. They probably would behave even worse if they had grades to flaunt. Still, if the ACMP's little self-test helps fellowship thrive in an art as close to the heart as music-making, we birders might gain by imitation. And—who knows?—maybe the swellheads would score B's.

The self-graded birder.

PAYING THE HOST

Tipping pro guides or tour leaders is awkward, as tips always are. Should we tip by the lifer? There must be a better way. As an amateur, I don't charge visitors for what is, after all, the pleasure of birding with them. I figure other hosts feel the same way, although the smart visitor does clear this up when planning the trip. Still, uncertainty can hover, usually revealed by darting eyes. As a host, I sense that visitors wonder about paying the day's costs; and as a visitor, I sense that hosts, too, wonder what to do. Here is how, over the years, I have come to deal with this matter:

AS A HOST. I *like* to go birding. About 90 percent of the gas I use during the day moves the car I was going to drive anyway; having another birder along takes only a few dimes more for gas. I pack my lunch, and I have passes that avoid daily entrance fees to parks, so there's no extra costs there, either. For visitors, "paying for the gas" is of course symbolic; but unless the day's trip is to an especially distant place, maybe it is a gesture that can be turned to better purpose.

When visitors offer to pay the day's costs, I suggest that, instead, they make a donation to a local environmental or birding group of their choice back home while the memory of our day is fresh. Most of the time they seem delighted with the idea. We have had a good day birding, and now birds and habitats somewhere will benefit. Everyone wins.

AS A VISITOR. If we are near civilization, I tell my host at the start of the day that I would like to get a deli sandwich for lunch and buy my host one, too. Also, I ask at the start to pay for gas and any entrance fees, because, despite what I said just above, these are still the expected gestures, and I am glad to make them. But at the end of the day I tell my host that I plan, as well, to make a donation to such-and-such an environmental or birding group, as thanks for our day. Again, the reaction always seems very positive. Again, everyone wins.

Could this be an idea whose time has come?

DISCONTENTS AND TONICS

When I asked a birder one morning if she had found any-thing special, she replied, "No . . . *not yet!*" As my wife, Louise, says, "You have to be an optimist to be a birder." But birding also has its doldrums. Here are three that I sail into now and then.

DOLDRUM 1: THE JADED BIRDER SYNDROME. For all the pleasure of sharing them, travelers' tales can bring on a cer-tain glumness. One friend, recently returned from Venezuela, remarked that she had seen more species in one tree there than we had found all morning. I brushed it off with a "that's-there-this-is-here" shrug. But local birding did seem rather tame for the next hour. Déjà vu the chickadees and the sparrows. I yearned for a rare bird or a long trip.

DOLDRUM 2: TOO MANY NO FLY ZONES. Wistfulness also hovers during quiet days and seasons. There is no denying the hush and lull that settle over the countryside on a hot summer afternoon, and the ennui that can over-take a birder sweltering there, or the desolation of a frozen marsh, or the emptiness of a deserted lake. Particularly if one is birding alone, any optimism that thrives in such situations has got to be pathological. It is fine enough to convert the day to a study day, but where are the birds to study?

DOLDRUM 3: DOUBTS. From time to time, especially when I am far from home (see page 56), but often enough at home, too, I stare at a young sparrow or a fall warbler or an *Empidonax* flycatcher, and I am stumped. I know we should all accept a few uncertainties in life, but sometimes I wonder if I am making any progress anymore. My friends seem to have gotten much sharper than I. So many birds, so little time.

Each of these three woes has antidotes. The first, the jaded birder syndrome, has a ready cure: I show these stale birds to visitors who have traveled far to meet my familiar species. Or I spend a day with an ardent beginner. The birders I escort on these days may think I am doing them a favor, but I am also treating myself to seeing familiar birds through new eyes. It always works.

Another cure for wistfulness: design and try out a birding route, a course, one that might produce a rousing list of species in a morning or even on a quiet afternoon, or adopt and monitor a birding patch of a few acres (see "A Patch of One's Own," page 51). Or make a list of fifty or sixty species in twenty different families and try to find them all in a morning. Chasing targets gives birding a wholly different feel from just visiting familiar habitats for "what's there."

By the same token, revisiting a patch of one's own through the circle of the seasons gives the familiar, local species continually renewed importance. And patches have an odd payoff: habitué that I have become there, sometimes I feel deliciously proprietary about the arboretum I have made my patch. It has become like my own estate even if the gates do stand open all day to others. Its bird list is shorter than a hot spot's, but strolling there month in and month out makes me feel like a birding baron.

As for the second of the birding doldrums, a birdless habitat, what on earth possessed you to go there anyway? But since you have, treat it as a seasonally crummy habitat (see page 29), and work it for surprises. Vagrant birds do turn up in forlorn places; give yourself a decent chance to find

. . . in one of birding's doldrums . . .

them before you move on. Or stay and switch your focus away from birds. For example, on a hot summer afternoon I seek butterflies, honorary birds. Or I watch dragonflies, which combine the challenge of tough, on-the-wing IDs with the joy of fascinating insect behavior. Sometimes I try identifying at least the families of a few other insects, or a few plants, at least until I start thinking, "They're nice, but they're not birds." Sometimes I pull out a hand lens and enter the very strange world of tiny creatures living on plants or in the debris atop the soil.

Sometimes on what seem to be birdless days I look about for animate and inanimate examples of nature's remarkably few basic patterns: spirals, explosions, branching patterns, meanders, lines of stress and flow, just a few polyhedrons . . . So many appearances, yet of so few patterns! (Some years ago Peter Stevens wrote a fascinating book, *Patterns in Nature*, that made me see them as if for the first time.) These forays can become field days within field days. Birds give us living focal points around which the rest of nature arranges itself. When the birds aren't there for us, all the rest of nature still is, filled with other marvels.

The third of my occasional disquiets is self-doubt. Weekend birders cannot hope to be much better than weekend golfers, who may score well on undemanding holes (for birders, ID'ing the easy species) but generally fold on the tough ones (for birders, ID'ing the bafflers). Adding field time, even in snatches, is still the surest way to achieve more birding skill and confidence. Birding does take skill; birding well demands diligent and frequent practice and lots of time. But unlike,

Sometimes
I wonder if I am making
progress anymore.

say, playing Beethoven, birding is not a craft of great profundity, even if a birder does reap profound rewards. I have already called it a kind of fluency. An identification quandary is like being at a loss for words. Fluency comes with using a language continually; to lay off is to get rusty. The same with birding: when I asked a varsity birder friend how often she birded, she replied, "I never stop."

Above all, to relieve the birding blahs, I seek the companionship of other birders. And as a special tonic, nowadays we can attend famous workshops on difficult groups—gull workshops, hawk and shorebird ones, even sparrow workshops. They give us chances to learn these birds with the major leaguers. These are the master classes of our craft. Or try to find a local mentor. A fine weaver I knew counseled novices and intermediates alike to apprentice to master weavers, because that is how the craft—any demanding craft—is best learned and best passed on. We seek tutors in music and art; why not in birding?

Too shy to ask for such special attention? Can't or won't go off to highfalutin faraway classes? Then join with others in local workshops about some troubling group of species. For example, every winter a dozen species and more than thirty plumages of gulls come to Monterey Bay and confound us locals. But almost every year the bird club I belong to saves us from discouragement by holding "Gull Therapy Sessions" led by local experts. We go to them with furrowed brows; we emerge from them refreshed in skill and spirit.

A PHILOSOPHICAL
INTERLUDE

ASKING QUESTIONS IN THE FIELD

We birders can always ask a bird the question "Who are you?" and move on. But if we try to ask our bird more than its name, if we try to be more than listers and twitchers, bird *watchers* instead of merely birders, we run the risk of a strange stand-off. Bereft of questions, we stare at birds; and birds, full of answers, if only we would ask, just stare back.

Birdwatching is a roving interview between people and birds that we can conduct whenever (but only when) our paths cross. An interview without questions is an oxymoron. So what questions might we ask that birds themselves, rather than our books at home, can answer? As my teacher and friend Donald Abbott patiently taught me, "When books and animals disagree, as they often do, the animal is always right." A keener challenge still: what questions can birds answer during just our brief encounters? Brevity drastically limits an interview. And hardest of all, what questions lead in a half hour or so to answers that do not start with "maybe"? The birds' own answers to our questions consist only of what we observe, not what we surmise. The great Yankee catcher Yogi Berra is said to have said, "You can observe a lot by watching." But all we can observe are the static and kinetic patterns that occur then and there. That is, something has to happen *while we watch.*

Except by inference, the interview cannot answer questions about evolution; that process takes a very long time and our interview is, above all, brief. We can observe only evolutionary moments. By the same token, the casual watcher cannot follow protracted processes in the life cycle, like growth and development, or track a species' movements through the years or the seasons, or even describe a bird's biology at other times of day than when it is encountered. (For example, the bird awake may not reveal where it sleeps.)

In a day, we cannot answer questions about evolution.

And as to a bird's behavior during our encounter, no matter how closely we watch what it does, we can only surmise the bird's mental state. The risk of misunderstanding besets us. No wonder our efforts at an interview are so frustrating.

We can investigate only the here and now, and we can ask only a little bit about even that. In a brief interview, we can ask the bird about its outward appearance and structure, its sounds, and its postures and movements; a little about the size and immediate distribution of the population it is part of (perhaps only a flock); a few questions about its current behavior; and a few more about its ecological surroundings. How we register the bird's answers reveals the kinds of questions we can ask about these topics: we can draw its appearance, record its sounds, film its movements, count its numbers, map its local distribution, describe (sometimes by clever diagrams) its behavior, and map or tally its habitat and close neighbors. That's it. This short list about exhausts our interrogative options as casual reporters. The bird's answers to the rest of what interests us will come only with far longer acquaintance than a day afield, or not from the bird at all but rather from books—but would the birds agree? Questions that ask why, provocative though they are, usually stop an interview with nature in its tracks. We know our quick interview has gone astray when the answers we think we have gotten from the bird all start with "maybe." For those sorts of answers are not the bird's; they are our own, about our conjecture. Then we have to try harder to honor the maxim "describe, don't explain."

So field-day questions must be modest. Some questions really are stupid, but *no question is too modest*. A canny interviewer poses modest questions one by one. If the questions are shrewd enough, their little answers will combine to tell a good story. While these answers measure an interview's progress, the questions are the engine that drives it and the wheel that steers it. When observational answers don't come quickly, when the interview seems to wander or stall, the problem probably lies with the questions.

Imagine interviewing some godwits on a mudflat. What can we ask these birds?

Q: How old are you?
A: Look at our plumage: what it says is all we'll tell you.

Q: Where have you come from and where are you going?
A: We aren't going to tell you while you watch us here and now.

Q: Why are your bills so long?
A: In this brief encounter, unless we start feeding (and maybe not even then) we aren't going to tell you that, either— not even whether their length is a help or a hinderance, any more than your nose's length may be.

Q: When you feed, how deeply do you plunge your bills into the mud?
A: Watch us.

Q: How do you find your food deep in the mud?
A: We just do, and for today that will have to do.

Q: When you probe the mud, is your bill closed or a little open?

A: Get the light just right and watch us closely. And while you're at it, watch our bill *tips*—and, just when our bills touch the mud, try to see our tongues!

Q: When you stand on one leg, do you switch legs now and then?

A: Watch us patiently.

Q: Is the leg you stand on the upstream or upwind one?

A: Wait and watch as the tide flows or the wind blows.

Q: When you sleep on one leg, which wing do you tuck your head under, compared to the leg you are standing on?

Ask questions the bird can answer.

A: Right now we are awake. You will have to catch us sleeping.

Q: Why do you stand on one leg, anyway? What does it gain
   you?
A: For now, we will tell you only that now and then we do.

Q: When one of you stands on one leg, many of you do.
   What is going on with this contagious behavior?
A: Well, why do you people yawn contagiously?

Here is the pattern: some questions the birds can answer
on the spot, some they will answer only slowly and over a
long program of observation, some send us to our book-
shelves, for better or worse, and some leave us analogizing
from other birds or in some other fashion opining or merely
wondering. Some questions drive our interview with the
birds forward, while others leave us interviewing only our
own thoughts or other's assertions.

Our interview proceeds by questions and answer-seek-
ing observations. Sometimes we make a nice observation, but
one that is relevant to a question we did not ask; now we have
an orphan answer. For example:

Q: Do individual godwits stand consistently on one leg or
   the other? That is, are they right-legged or left-legged?
A: They seem to twist about on whatever leg they stand on.

A nice observation, but it does not answer the question;
it answers a different question. Or:
A (let's say): They stand on the upwind leg.

The same difficulty: a nice observational answer to another question. Disconnects like these happen surprisingly often in the fluidity of fieldwork. When they do, I file my observations in hopes that eventually, as answers, they may find a more apt question. (In this example, the more apt questions might be "Do godwits *do* anything when they stand on one leg?" and "Does the wind affect how a godwit stands on one leg?") Then I go back to the question I did ask and try again to observe its answer. On interview days, the best questions keep company with the best observations, but sometimes I have to act the matchmaker.

TELLING OBSERVATIONS
FROM INTERPRETATIONS

Our simplest observations are shot through with interpretations. Even seeing a bird as a bird at all is an act of interpretation. "Oh come on!" you cry. But here is personal evidence:

- I walked right by a Common Poorwill; I mistook its body for leaves.

- After much searching, I almost stepped on a Snowy Plover that blended into the beach sand.

- I failed to make an oriole out of fragments half hidden in the foliage. I have also done the converse: made leaves into an oriole, right down to its sex.

Mistaking objects for birds, life-giving bloopers.

🐦 I mistook (and not for the first time) a decoy for a duck—although it did bob strangely.

🐦 A friend and I had almost ID'd two wren-like birds hopping on a shade-dappled forest log, when they twitched in unison; they were the ear-tips of a deer lying behind the log.

🐦 And in the past few years I have tried to turn buoys into alcids, weathervanes into falcons, trash bags into egrets, the stump of a tree limb into a Barn Owl, old cow pies into young longspurs, four twists of blue surveyor's tape into four Mountain Bluebirds—life-giving bloopers all.

These embarrassing episodes ought to persuade any birder that identifications are fraught with risky interpretations, fallible observations, and hard questions, all in intricate interplay. In *Art and Illusion*, Ernst Gombrich puts the matter this way: "Every observation . . . is a result of a question we ask nature, and every question implies a tentative hypothesis. We look for something because our hypothesis makes us expect certain results." That's exactly how I got into each of my little misadventures, and how I got out of them, too.

James Elkins, in *The Object Stares Back*, applies Gombrich's scenario to all of seeing. Seeing, he stresses, is not a passive absorption of the visual world, but rather an active, intense act. Our brain radically edits the visual glut our eyes take in, and then radically rebuilds the coherent scene we "see." At one point, Elkins says: "My world is full of holes. . . . The way I see is a little the way a blind man taps along the street: he knows just that one spot where his cane touches down, and he hopes he can pretty much guess the rest."

Seeing observing is interrogative, selective, and interpretive from the start. Noticing that poorwill or that plover is merely a case in point. But maybe we can draw a distinction between the *claims* we make when we observe and those we make when we interpret our observations. That they are so tightly connected, each testing our hold on the other, is all the more reason to try to tell them apart. The great biologist C. B. van Niel used to distinguish his own claims this way: "When someone asks me that awful question, 'And . . . how do you know?', if I start to point, it was probably an observation. If I start to sweat, it was certainly an interpretation."

A hypothesis is an interpretation made logically formal. A robust hypothesis puts itself at risk by making testable predictions about what will happen in such-and-such a situation. If our observations then contradict those predictions, the hypothesis itself is in serious trouble. Some sciences, like particle physics and molecular biology, thrive on lightning-bright hypotheses, razor-sharp predictions, and clean, sometimes elegant, observational tests of those predictions and hence of the hypotheses themselves. But they are a far cry from natural history. Naturalists, meticulous birdwatchers among them, contrive hypotheses, too, about "what's happening" (and how and why). But the predictions that follow and the observations that might test them often lead naturalists to messy, "more-or-less" answers, sometimes couched in statistics, instead of neat yesses or nos. Out where the wild things live, if we go beyond IDs and *observe* birds, we encounter multiple causes and effects, layered interactions, and other explanatory monsters. To top off this complexity, what we have found out may apply only to this or that species or to a specific time and place, to be generalized at our peril. Laws of life, they are not; they are more like somewhat bigger puzzle-pieces than we started with. It sounds to me like the world of the white cane.

Just as Elkins's blind man knows only the ground he actually taps, so also, as a birdwatcher, I try not to interpret too grandly from what I observe. I think our canniest goal is not how much we can claim to have learned from an observation, but rather how little. Let's call it the strategy of least lessons: what is the *least* lesson our observation teaches?

Guided by this modesty, we will not make grand discoveries, but who goes birding for them? Little interpretive claims are surprisingly forceful ones if we can test them then and there against our observations.

When we simply identify birds, we make these least interpretive claims: it's a Savannah Sparrow, a Herring Gull. They are hypotheses with predictions, so to speak, that can be tested by a second look at the bird. When we go beyond identification, things quickly get more strenuous; at first, drawing even the least lessons may confound us, but so do most new skills.

A few pages ago I contrived a little interview with some godwits. Using it and taking my cue from Gombrich, I can make hypotheses that generate predictions and hence the questions and observations that test them. For example:

Hypothesis: The birds are in their first year.
Prediction: A distinctive, first-year plumage. Looking at their plumage should confirm or contradict this prediction.

Hypothesis: They are going to Mexico.
Prediction: None that I can test by any immediate observation. Maybe a banding and recovery program would do that over the next few weeks.

Hypothesis: Their long bills let them feed more deeply in the mud than most other shorebirds.
Prediction: They will do exactly that, poke the full length of their bills into the mud, reaching food other shorebirds with shorter bills cannot. And sometimes they do exactly that, face against mud. But they probe less deeply, too.

How does this mix of observations bear on my hypothesis? Maybe I need to refine my hypothesis and its predictions.

And so, by the little steps and missteps of observing, by contriving little hypotheses, by making predictions from them, and then by testing them against new observations, I make my way toward some fuller understanding of these birds in their world.

WATCHING GULLS AND DOING SCIENCE

One of winter's delights here is watching gulls that spend hours each day riding a stream across a hundred feet of beach to the sea. They fly up the beach, drop into the stream, and float its length. Many of them bathe (well, at least they flap about) on their improbable little trips, but many simply bob along, like so many haphazard boats. Other gulls stand alongside and seem to watch the ones that go by. Are the gulls that float along playing, as ravens seem to play when they slide down snowy slopes? Behavioral observations are notoriously colored by interpretations. It is bad enough when we try to report a bird's overt behavior without loaded terms. But when we try to enter the bird's mind to grasp its mental state, matters only get worse. Then, if someone asks me, "And . . . how do you know?" I find myself not so much in a sweat as at a loss.

"Play" implies a state of mind. Ironically, for a long time minds have been strictly off limits to investigators of animal behavior. The stricture has the force of a taboo. Overt

Gulls at play.

behavior is fair investigative game, but what produces it other than physiology is not. When it comes to science, this distinction persists for good reason. As Alexander Skutch puts it in *The Minds of Birds*, we "know" other creatures' mental states (such as pleasure, fear, concentration, sociability, playfulness, tenderness) only by intuition, inferring their psyches from our own. Perhaps our inferences are accurate, perhaps they are irresistibly commonsensical, but they can appeal to no test beyond a personal one: "How would *I* feel?" Intuition leaves us stranded outside rational explanation, knowing and yet not knowing. Our heart knows our dog loves us, but our science doesn't. In science, we cannot get far in understanding a phenomenon whose very existence we know only nonrationally, even if intensely. Surely birds have minds! But when it comes to science (uniquely, I think), we feel the harsh truth of Wolfgang Pauli's dismissal: an idea that can't be tested isn't even wrong.

So my observation of those gulls, its lessons obscure, stands as an unexplained—even inexplicable—anecdote. Scientists (I am one) tend to disparage anecdotes: "It's just an anecdote." It is not the accuracy of the report so much as its investigative worth that is called into question. Anecdotes report mere opportunistic peeks into birds' lives. But if the observations behind them are impeccable, we would seem to be poorer for passing anecdotes by and richer for taking them seriously, even if we are not sure what to make of them. If that is so, then why don't scientists welcome our anecdotes?

In contrast to the folkways of anecdotes, powerful formal customs of language and method govern generally acceptable scientific descriptions of nature's patterns and processes. One of them is Galileo's old dictum that "the lan-

Why don't scientists welcome anecdotes?

guage of nature is number." For Galileo, nonnumerical attributes are private human perceptions (Is my red your red?), not public natural qualities. Making or testing hypotheses, so central to explanatory science, depends on a public language ("red's" agreed-upon spectral wavelength, a numerical measurement) to state its claims and predictions. By themselves, words too often fail us; the clearest of words are full of nuances and so mean different things to different people. In contrast, numbers "just mean what they say."

Numbers have a public clarity, as do (or can) their analogues like equations and some other diagrams; they provide science's hypothesis-stating language of choice. The success of this choice has been so thorough, it is an understandable surmise that we must be able to turn our observations into number or some other language of publicly testable hypotheses, or maybe we aren't doing science after all. Anecdotes, so verbal, usually fail this test. Anecdotes report news but mostly do not lend themselves to the particular sort of news analysis we recognize as science. They can lead to science, but they cannot get there by themselves. And so, to many scientists' ways of thinking, natural history, steeped as it is in anecdote, narrative as it is in its traditions, fails Pauli's test. In *Why Birds Sing*, David Rothenberg sums it up nicely: much of the grand tradition of natural history, he writes, "falls somewhere in the valley between science and poetry."

Masterly hands, though, do mold anecdotes into marvelous science, and despite Galileo's dictum, into science with words, not numbers, as its central language. Niko Tinbergen—much more than a casual birdwatcher!—combined observations and experiments to reveal the mechanics and subtleties of the Herring Gull's complex social behavior. He deciphered how these birds recognize one another, how they pair up for breeding, how the parent's bill prompts its chick's feeding, and how the interplay of many other signals and largely innate responses guide a bird's activities. Through this long program of research, Tinbergen stoutly resisted the lure of intuiting his birds' mental states. He did not reject their existence; he simply stuck to demonstrable findings about their behavior, which were news enough. Konrad Lorenz's studies of Eurasian Jackdaws, Bernd Heinrich's of Common Ravens, and David Lack's of Common Swifts are other examples of research that transformed anecdotes into systematic interpretations. They have taught me precious lessons not only about natural history as science but also about how to watch birds.

This long reconnaissance brings us back to watching those gulls. The physicist Werner Heisenberg made this tremendous statement: "What we observe is not nature itself, but nature exposed to our method of questioning." My winter gulls' mental state lies beyond our familiar scientific methods of questioning. But to doubt, for this reason, the very existence of other creatures' mentality is to confuse method (or in this case our very lack of it) with reality, the very distinction Heisenberg draws. How, then, can we reconcile what our hearts know about the minds of birds with what our heads dictate about the methods of science?

Before Newton and Leibniz, scarcely three hundred years ago, there was no calculus, and modern statistics dates from the twentieth century. Once devised, these languages joined the tradition of logic to shape most of contemporary science. Nowadays they frame almost all of its questions, organize its observational data, and express its interpretive answers. For many scientists, they have set the terms by which we expose nature to our questioning. But the terms are not so very old, compared, say, to most of philosophy's. Most sciences are in their youth, even if it is the regained youth of newly adopted paradigms. There will be a twenty-second-century science—even a twenty-fifth-century one, about as far ahead of us as the Scientific Revolution is behind us. I like to imagine that by then we will have devised new ways to probe the conundrum of the mind, to expose it to new ways of scientific questioning. I cannot believe that in its short life, science has already mustered all the languages and methods it ever will.

Deciphering the mentality of birds awaits the languages and methods of a science yet to come. Already we are emerging from the thrall of behaviorism. Taboos against anthropomorphism have begun to give way to the bright prospect of newly tolerant, yet rigorously disciplined inquiries into animal behavior and, yes, into the minds of birds. Who would have thought that watching gulls at play could have brought us to such a philosophical pass!

THE OCEAN OF AIR

"The ocean of air," so often invoked as a metaphor, describes a very real thing. The earth's air really does form an ocean, as much as the marine waters do; an aerial ocean wraps the globe. Gaseous air is as much a fluid as liquid water is, just less dense. Winds are currents; downwind is downstream. Some pilots talk of their planes swimming through the air. We walk on the bottom of this sea of air, as much as crabs walk on the bottom of their sea of water. Perhaps crabs look up at swimming fish the way we do at flying birds.

At middle latitudes this aerial sea is six to seven miles deep. It is where the weather is. Above it are ozone shields and northern lights and the uppermost jet streams, but for the most part not much weather and not much air. When we fly across the continent at thirty-seven thousand feet, we fly mostly above the weather—give or take a thunderhead charging into the stratosphere—and we fly mostly above the air. The sea of air may seem deep when we look up into it from the ground, but when we look down at the ground from a coast-to-coast plane, we can sense how shallow it really is. Birds, "creatures of the air" though they are, live close to the bottom of this aerial sea. When we approach an airport, we reenter the world of birds only as the flight attendant says, "Bring your seat backs to their full upright position."

How does the atmosphere's roughly six-mile depth compare to the expanse of the landscape we live on? When it comes to big pictures, I need dimensions I can grasp. So this question sent me to a map of North America, one in which the three thousand miles from San Francisco to New York City measured five feet. On such a map, six hundred miles is a foot, and so fifty miles is an inch. Six miles, then, is about an eighth of an inch. On a map of America five feet across,

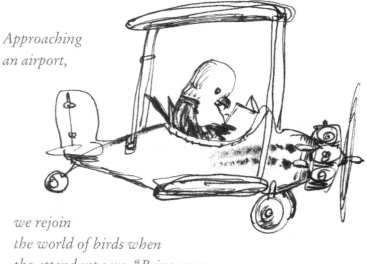

*Approaching
an airport,*

*we rejoin
the world of birds when
the attendant says, "Bring your
seat backs to their full upright position."*

the six-mile-deep ocean of air above it is only an eighth of an inch thick, like a pane of window glass. Here was a comparison I could handle. And, surprised by it, now I could believe that what living things do in the marine realm and on land might well affect such a shallow atmosphere, if they do it often and widely enough, and if in so doing they pour by-product gases into the air. Over geological eons, photosynthesis by tiny planktonic plants oxygenated first the earth's waters and then the overlying atmosphere. Since the Industrial Revolution, as we have burned fossil fuels in prodigious quantities, we, too, have altered the very chemistry of the global atmosphere.

At the bottom of the ocean of air, where we live, terrestrial habitats invite analogy with submarine ones. The air's birds are akin to the waters' fishes. Our woods and gardens are to the land what coral reefs are to the marine sea bottom. Shrubs and trees provide big structures with living surfaces, and they compete for advantage among themselves as much as corals do. Songbirds are like little reef fish that dart in and out of cover. In the marine and aerial sea alike, swift carnivores—the reef's more ravenous fish, the woodlot's accipiter hawks—patrol these patchy refuges, snatching the careless. Still bigger predators float in open water near the bottom and search it for their food, the way airborne harriers and buteos scour the ground. Analogies, all.

Why bother with metaphors and analogies? Because they are the threads we use to sew together the fabrics of our comprehended world. Treacherous though they may be, analogies and metaphors inform before they betray. They do more than help us make our first sense of the unfamiliar; they help us see the familiar afresh. Proust said, "The real voyage of discovery consists not in seeking new landscapes but in having new eyes." Analogies and metaphors seem to free up mental anchors and so can lead our most ordinary musings into Proustian voyages of discovery.

Here is a story that provides both a metaphor and an analogy. In "Who We Are," I wrote about how a few geese, a flock of finches, an invasion of swifts, a tree full of warblers, and a meadowlark combined to change me one spring from a rather aimless boarding-school boy into an ardent birder. The meadowlark really did the trick. It leapt up at my feet, and it dumbfounded me. For a long time after it flushed, I stood in that field, transfixed by the image of that bird in flight. The analogy: as a turning kaleidoscope's colored glass chips fall into new and beautiful patterns, so also, over that spring, had the pieces of my young world. The meadowlark gave the kaleidoscope its definitive twist. I watched the bird fly away, and when I turned I saw the world with new eyes. And the metaphor: lightning had struck. I can still recall the shock of it. I walked back to my dormitory a different boy, and I knew it. Many lifelong birders report such startling initiations, many of them on occasions as mundane as mine. (For the newsman John Kieran, it was seeing a nuthatch inch down a fence post.) Only metaphors and analogies can cope with their importance.

Here is another occasion, one framed from the start in the terms of a metaphor. In college, long since a birder but now contemplating natural history as a career, I read Evelyn Hutchinson's famous essay, *The Ecological Theater and the Evolutionary Play*. Habitats, he wrote, are ecological theaters, each presenting its version of the same drama of natural selection, the same evolutionary play. Each habitat, each ecological theater, has its own scenery and players and impromptu plot, but the same great play unfolds in all of them. Of course! No wonder I wanted to be a naturalist! As we birders make our rounds, we become an intimate audience in the theater of ecology, witness to moments in the play of evolution itself. As much as my meadowlark, Hutchinson's metaphor gave me new eyes through which I have looked at nature, even at the air itself, ever since.

SKILLS

GETTING ON THE BIRD

Rustiness after a few weeks away from birding hits me in three ways: unsettling hesitations about some of my IDs, "lazy ear" (see "Listening" page 96), and trouble in woodlands getting on birds at all with the naked eye. While I was away, the trees seem to have grown an awful lot of rustling, scintillating leaves, especially overhead. A bird once spotted, I raise and aim my binoculars as smoothly as ever, but for a while I cannot figure out where to look. "Where? Where?" becomes a mantra.

I have asked many birders about this problem of getting onto birds, and many report that they share it and are as puzzled as I am about how to deal with it. I once asked for online help on BirdChat but got more commiseration than practical advice. When BirdChat fails to solve my problem, I know it is a big one. The best suggestion turned on searching trees with one's eyes slightly out of focus, perhaps to broaden the field of scrutiny. After a fashion, this works; I do then pick up movements more widely, if blurrily. But those avian

Search with eyes slightly out of focus.

specks slip all too quickly back into the foliage, and so I have to resume my search all over again.

Another helpful hint when searching for songbirds has been to seek the flock, then the bird. Especially out of breeding season, many birds tend to group together, even if only loosely. Locating these roving flocks and sticking with them, sorting through what are often more birds than was first apparent, rewards the patient birder, as one bird leads the eye to another. A third suggestion has been to remember that the bird's little movements in the foliage will reveal it to the birder who waits tenaciously without moving at all. Sometimes this does not work: try to find that loud but stone-still Ovenbird. But even these birds must move eventually. Not so, of course, the ptarmigans, stones with eyes.

After a time off from birding, my remedy has been to be patient, because naked-eye keenness seems to return soon enough in the field. But for the beginner it must be a continuing hell—do you remember?—seeking small birds in big trees. This syndrome may account for some of the exasperating occasions when companions seem almost willfully unable to see what we are pointing out. And it suggests we can afford to make our directions as clear as possible, and more ample than "There it is! *There!*" When birding alone, we can practice directing imaginary companions to birds. For example, we can turn the tree into a huge clock and put the bird on its hour. We can trace a verbal path from our feet to the bird. We can point with a well-bent arm or deftly aim a mirror (see "Mirrors" page 168), narrating all the while. Doing this *out loud* is essential; only then can one hear one's ambiguous or botched directions. *Sotto voce*, they all sound fine. If nonbirding passersby stop and smile, I point the bird out to them, just for the practice.

Some birders do not stay resolutely enough on a bird after getting on it. Confronted with a mixed flock, they keep switching their attention from one bird to another. Psychology defeats ophthalmology. In that situation, it takes discipline to stick with the one bird we think merits our closest attention. And like any good intention, it can backfire. In Big Bend recently, I met a very disciplined birder who had hiked to the heights to see that prize, a Colima Warbler. He did see one, but he refused to be distracted (despite the pleas of a dozen beside-themselves observers) by a Flame-colored

Tanager in the very next tree. For every calamity like that, though, I can recall ten when a birder's attention wandered too soon, and to a common species, and the bird of the day got away.

Birding with companions, we can divvy up a flock and share our finds by calling them out. The more fluent we get, the less distraction intrudes as we focus with ease now on this bird, now on that one—smooth shifts of close attention, subtle and flexible. Layoffs compromise that touch, that fluency. There is only one remedy: go birding more often.

RAISING AND AIMING BINOCULARS

It might seem an elementary matter, but a surprising number of birders who can get on the bird—who can pick up with their naked eyes the speck everyone is shouting about—then have trouble getting their binoculars on it. This is especially a problem with birds in trees. Some people habitually aim their binoculars askew and have to train themselves out of this habit. Even then, some woodland birders find that the foliage that ought to provide markers only makes matters worse. Birds flitting through the treetops often appear for only an instant, then vanish as they go about their lofty business. Problems aiming and focusing binoculars—especially high-powered ones with a commensurately narrow field of view or shallow depth of focus—can ruin encounter after encounter. When it comes to raising and aiming and focusing binoculars, here are three maneuvers that can help.

MANEUVER 1. Locate the bird among neighboring landmarks such as a particular interplay of branches or leaves or a distinctive twig or a patch of light. Then aim and focus at that, not at the bird itself. That is, aim and focus at the large and stationary frame of reference where the bird is, not at the tiny, moving bird itself. The bird may be hidden or may have moved, but at least you know you are looking where you meant to.

A little bird in a big tree is much too small a target to aim at. Use your binocs as though you were throwing a net around the bird. This is especially important if your quarry is flitting about unpredictably, or if there are twigs and leaves that let you see it only in bits and pieces, or if it has found a thick branch to creep behind. Aim and focus for the place, not the bird. If the bird has not left, it is there. At least, that is where you last saw it.

MANEUVER 2. The major leaguer Jeff Kingery taught me this: Keeping your eyes on the bird, first raise your binoculars to face level but hold them vertically (that is, aimed straight down at the ground), so your thumbs rest against your cheekbones. Then rotate the binocs to your eyes as if they were hinged to your cheeks. Now look through them.

This way, what was a single movement extending over two feet becomes two movements: first the big vertical one of raising the binocs from your chest to your face, then just a little rotation at the face to actually aim them with delicate control. These two motions, raise and rotate, combine to look and feel like one. So did the fast draws of Wild West gunslingers. First they whisked their pistols out of their holsters,

*Focus on the place,
not the bird.*

then they aimed and fired: two motions, even if blurred into
one by their lightning speed. But *don't* imitate their lightning
speed if you don't want the bird to run for cover. Raise and
rotate with deliberation—in effect, not letting the bird know
what you are up to. Think molasses.

Raising and rotating has another advantage for birders:
it keeps the binoculars' two big, round, staring eyes aimed
down toward the ground unless you are actually looking

through them. And if you keep your binocs vertically "in neutral" but still at your face, just rotating them in and out of action as needed, they will serve you in still another way: they will partly cover your own bird-alarming eyes.

MANEUVER 3. If you can't find a half-hidden bird almost at once in your binoculars, start over. Ordinarily, do not try to search foliage with binoculars. Rotate them back down to neutral against your cheeks or lower them entirely to your chest, and then search again by naked eye for the bird and its markers.

If you can't find the bird in your binoculars, for all you know it has flown away. Or you could be looking at the wrong markers. Searching through binoculars is like searching through a paper-towel tube; that foot-long tube's tiny field of view (FOV) about equals that of 10X binoculars. Yes! Look through that tube and be shocked! Don't waste time searching by tunnel vision. Regroup. With your binocs in neutral, peer over them to re-find the bird, note anew the interplay of close markers, and try again.

And here is a further thought: if you habitually lose track of birds in trees, could your binoculars themselves be partly to blame? "Good carpenters don't blame their tools," but lots of birders use binoculars (especially compacts, but also high-powered full-size ones) with small FOVs; think again of looking through that paper-towel tube. Moderately close birds can leave a narrow FOV entirely just by flitting about. Lately I have backed off from 10X to 8X to gain greater FOV and depth of focus. Some major leaguers I know use 7X optics for this same reason. Birders who frequent the Eastern forests often use 7X binoculars. Much of their viewing is from hemmed in places like forest paths, at close quarters (where of course any binoculars have a narrower FOV than they do at a greater distance), and into veritable jumbles of foliage, all of which are circumstances that make a broad FOV desirable. The rest of us can learn from them as we seek birds in less confined or confusing habitats.

But don't we need the power? As our identification skills grow, we tend less and less to laboriously scrutinize every bird's every detail, or we leave that to scopes (say, to examine a nearby shorebird's individual feathers or a distant hawk's tail). To make most straightforward IDs, we focus instead on larger traits: shape, proportions, particular but entire feather groups, behavior, sounds, and so on. And when we do concentrate on the smallest observable details of the puzzlers, our experience somehow seems to provide the extra "magnification" our binoculars may lack. We still see details, but we have learned to select what to look at closely, and we pick them up by the play of light as much as by just staring at them. We see more because we know what to focus on. When our binocs are not up to the optical task, we can turn to a scope in some habitats or in others to strategies like pishing or luring more technologically or stalking. The rest of the time, which is just about all of the time, a wide FOV serves us best.

It is worth remembering, too, that a great deal of what powerful binoculars provide is psychological: the gratuitously dramatic view. We realize this with a jolt when we aim our binocs even at birds that are too close to focus on. The extraordinary close-up is always a thrill, but why not just look?

STANDING STILL

Canny birders stand still. In a scene in his video series *The Life of Birds*, David Attenborough walks quietly along a woodland path. Birds call in alarm all around him. From the treetops, he looks like a cat on the prowl. That is what we birders do, we prowl, and so we alarm our neighbors and we alarm the birds. What we see up close are mostly the fool-hardy birds, as anyone who was sitting there before we came along can tell us. The rest have taken cover. When we enter a habitat, we have to let it recover from the shock of our arrival. The birds there know from the very look of us that we are on a hunt. They must size us up before they dare to get on with their chores. To let them do that, we have to stand still, to glue both feet to the ground, to be as fixed and as silent as a statue, and in that slow way to join the habitat. Yet remarkably few birders seem to be able to do this. Another bird distracts: resist! An ear itches: resist! A fly bothers: resist! A thought reaches your mouth: be still!

Standing still has another advantage besides its calming effect. Where birds lurk within confusing thickets of branches and leaves, standing still gives our eyes a chance to take in the arrangements of light and shadow, of line and mass. This takes time. Pretty soon we become aware of moving clues that we would miss if we, too, were moving. Now

Standing still.

they move against a stationary background. And some of those moving clues are birds.

Standing still pays another dividend if you are birding by ear and listening. When we stop moving, an internal, physiological silence emerges. The cranial thud that every footfall makes, the slightly muffling gyres of air swirling in the hollows of our ears, the nostril noises that even non-wheezers make when exerting—all these interfere with hearing very faint noises around us. And with every step, our rustling clothes raise sonic walls around our bodies. "Stopping to listen" means just that.

But though standing still is easy enough advice, for many of us it is very hard to do for more than a few minutes; it can feel like an eternity. And sustaining a stalker's focus as we do it is harder still. If our body cannot wander, our mind tries to. This is why wild creatures so easily outwait us. They hold still; we don't. They bide their time; we spend ours. And in nature, when we stand still and "nothing happens," we tend to spend our time stingily, lest we waste it. Soon enough, we lose patience and want to get on with the day. In nature, it is as though we simply hang up the phone whenever we are put on hold.

One summer morning in the Utah desert, I stopped beside a pool and bent over a bear's paw print in the mud. A tiny frog had jumped into the pool as I arrived. I stood there watching the frog and the frog floated there watching me. After five silent, immobile minutes went by and "nothing happened," I hung up on nature and started on my way. A dozen paces on, I turned and looked back at the pool. The little frog, triumphant, was sitting in my wet footprint.

I know of no cure for losing patience with nature—with *nature*!—short of a revolutionary change of attitude. But we can make ourselves slow our pace. For example, I have added a featherweight, three-legged folding campstool to my back-pack, and I use it. The lowered head, the nicely bent knees and suddenly weightless feet, the body's acknowledgment of having come to a halt—whatever the physical cause, in my experience sitting comfortably in nature works wonders. The habitat slowly puts aside its stage-set air, creatures resume their lives, impatience quietly withdraws. Like a spell, a dif-ferent rhythm descends. With it, this thought stirs: "Maybe I should stay here awhile." Not the revolution, maybe, but at least its breath.

LISTENING

Listen. We can hear what we cannot see. We can recognize what we hear. As aural skills build, they add enormously to the enjoyment of birding. Listening is especially important and rewarding when birding in leafy habitats, but it also pays off in the open, because it lets us bird in a "multitasking" way, by eye and by ear at the same time, staying on one bird with one sense, on another with the other. This might seem to compound confusion in the field, but it doesn't. It simplifies. Using our ears knowledgeably lets us stay visually on a puzzling bird while identifying other birds by the sounds that come from behind us or from the side or emanate from cover. Conversely, we can concentrate our ears on a song or a call even as we survey our surroundings with our eyes. I admit that when I started birding as a kid, I wanted to avoid the discouragements that go along with first efforts to bird by ear. Eventually I learned better. Our ears can match our eyes, skill for skill, if only we persevere optimistically— or tenaciously.

Some birders scarcely listen to many open-habitat birds that they could, with a little practice, include in their aural acquaintance: ducks, swallows, many shorebirds. But when it comes to the summer woodland birds we often cannot see, listening is crucial. The Eastern beech-maple forests, for example, raise fortress walls of foliage around every summer clearing, and in the woods themselves the foliage closes overhead in multilevel canopies. The birds that dwell in these porous depths show themselves visually only as silhouettes against the sky's glare or as the merest bits of flitting plumage.

Listen.

And yet the summer woods echo with their songs and calls, fully and repeatedly presented for our scrutiny. Repeatedly is right: one dogged counter has reported that between sunrise and sunset on a summer day, a Red-eyed Vireo, that all-day singer of the Appalachian woods, delivered its lazy phrases over twenty-two thousand times.

Learning to identify birds by their sounds does present some problems that go well beyond the birds themselves. Visual creatures that we are, we insist that "seeing is believing" and warn ourselves, "Don't believe everything you hear"—hardly encouragement. What we see tends to linger as an afterimage, which we can even caress with our mind's eye. Sounds too often vanish as fast as they appear; musicians aside, we don't caress much at all with our ears, even though sounds caress us. To make matters worse, our language, so rich in visual vocabulary, struggles to describe sounds. Try describing some natural sounds without just pointing to other sounds that are like them ("It sounds like a . . ."). All this constraint complicates learning to identify birds by their sounds. If we cannot talk about them easily to others, we cannot think about them to ourselves, either. Even so, there are ways to make a start.

The first step is to separate the signal from the noise, to focus on a particular sound among the many out there. We do it all the time with visual signals—at a glance, so to speak—but not so often with what we hear. "What's that? . . . Listen . . . There it goes again." This focus contends with the confusion of the morning bird chorus or the rumble of traffic or the rustle of leaves or even, for God's sake, birders around us talking. It is a matter of noticing sounds at all. After a long layoff from birding, I need a day in the field to regain the knack of registering and sorting all the sounds that come at me at once. During that re-acquaintance with birds' sounds, I make my ears plod up and down through the octaves and concentrate on one pattern after another. Gradually, like eyes getting used to the light, my ears begin again to take in the rich acoustical scene.

What sounds? The tracker Jon Young sorts bird sounds into just a few utilitarian roles: claiming territory, courting mates, begging parents, spreading an alarm, and holding a flock together. Traditionally we distinguish songs from calls. In many ways it is an arbitrary matter or one of degree: a bird's songs are usually more complex than its calls—though not always (think of a chickadee's). And some people speak of all bird sounds as songs or as calls, but this fudges a useful distinction. Birds that do sing put their songs and their calls to very different purposes, so we must tell them apart in order to understand much about them. Songbirds sing to seduce mates and to announce their claims on breeding territories. At dawn many birds make their territorial rounds. They announce their presence afresh and listen for (and recognize as such) tolerable neighbors and trespassing strangers. Then they settle down to the day's business of singing erotic songs. Birds' songs are about sex and real estate; the rest, they leave to their calls.

Songs are birds' music; calls are birds' words. One bird-song authority, Charles Hartshorne, described calls as unmusical, rather unorganized, not rhythmical, "short, almost patternless, and the opposite of pure tones." And, he said, they are "tied much more directly to the immediately practical" than songs are. Its brief work done, a call stops, but songs go on and on as long as the hormones last. Both sexes call, and all year long, while mostly (but not always) it is the males that sing, and mostly just seasonally. Songs and calls differ, too, in that birds respond largely to their own species' songs, but to the calls of many other species besides their own. The more one examines them, the more calls and songs stand in contrast to each other.

If birds' calls were words, they would be almost entirely interjections and expletives: Wow! Hurrah! Whee! Eek! Damn! Yum! Hi! Oh! Ooh! Aah! Ow! Uh-oh ... And with these, a smattering of brisk commands: C'mon! Mine! Go away! Freeze! Go get 'em! Outa my way! Let me in! Feed me! Let's cuddle! Gotcha! Help! And from time to time a calling bird asks, "Where are you?" or—what amounts to the same thing—it says, "I am here."

An anthropological aside: It seems to me that "I am here" is one of the universal messages of speech. Birds sing it, horses whinny it, dogs bark it, people say it in every imaginable disguise. Eavesdrop, and very often that is all you will hear on all sides: people saying to each other, "I am here." In fact, I am inclined to believe that the secret to the animals' languages that Polynesia the Parrot taught the good John Dolittle, M.D., was that most of the time, most other animals, just like most people, are saying to each other simply, "I am here."

"I am here."

Hartshorne summed up calls as "snarls, growls, whines, meows, squeals, grunts, chirps, and squeaks" that contend with circumstances. Calls do not convey thoughts or reflect on ideas. They serve as a language of emotions and reactions; from them we infer (and, I think, so do other birds) the caller's panic, fear, anger, assertiveness, tentativeness, sexual arousal, hunger, confusion, loss, tenderness, irritation, contentment, pleasure, companionship, exhilaration. For Rosemary Jellis, calls express, in sum, "moods and events."

We humans utter a few innate, instinctive calls, too, as when we cry in distress or laugh in pleasure. I think we hear the voice of our instincts, too, in the theater's gasps and the stadium's cheers. Infants' babbling is an instinctive behavior, whatever the babbles' acquired accents. Probably even the act of speaking is biologically inherited, beneath its cultural veneer of linguistic imitation. By the same token, many of our interjections ("wow" and the rest) seem to me to be cultural words for innate calls. Wordless, birds have kept on calling.

If birds' calls deal with this much emotional freight, then each bird ought to have a variety of them. And they do. So why do we hear so few? One reason may be that we encounter individual birds so briefly. We tend to hear them as they cope with only one event, their encounter with us. We cross paths, and that's that. So we tend to know birds merely as anonymities that embody species: "It's a robin." But they *are* distinct individuals, each leading a unique life, each with its surprising personality, each with its vocabulary, as everyone who has raised wild birds tells us. Just as tourists see little of the lives of the locals they come upon—little of what is really going on, say, in that foreign village—so also with birders and birds. Spotting the birds is the quick part; entering their lives as more than a disturbance takes much longer.

To me, calls are more fascinating than songs, because I feel I am really listening to the bird as it copes with life. Songs seem so . . . so public. But songs are what we hear most (in season, anyway) and they are one of nature's marvels. In the spring, we hear birdlife's opera. An angel descending from the sky upon a springtime earth would hear an arc of bird-song stretching from the tundra to the tropics as dawn and its chorus swept westward round and round the world. And in those weeks anyone, angel or not, who goes out before the sun rises can hear this same arc as it comes through the land-scape. I can recall how, long ago, when I first went birding at dawn in the Appalachian hills, I felt I could actually hear this astounding chorus arrive from the east, sustain a crescendo for an hour, and then rush on toward the west.

In the spring, we hear birdlife's opera.

Compared to a call, what is a song? Rosemary Jellis, in *Bird Sounds and Their Meaning*, distinguishes song by its element of "pattern and elaboration." "Even when a song is short, simple, and constructed of call-notes," she writes, "there is usually a firmer pattern in the sequence of sounds, a greater elaboration than in repeated calls; an obvious grouping of notes into phrases with predictable pauses between them and greater regularity of repetition." In *Born to Sing*, Charles Hartshorne describes calls as quick and sporadic, while songs, whether brief or lengthy, are persistent and repetitive. These characterizations may bring thrushes and orioles to mind, but even Henslow's Sparrow's "tiny set of notes," which lasts only half a second, meets Hartshorne's criterion of a song.

When we think of birdsong, we think mostly of the perching birds, and among them especially of the oscine families, such as vireos, thrushes, finches, warblers, orioles, sparrows, and tanagers: the so-called true songbirds. To avoid a circular argument, taxonomists, while recognizing the complexity of songbirds' voice-boxes, base this clan not on singing behavior so much as on such nonvocal traits as the windpipe's musculature, the foot's structure, an odd preening gland on the rump, and even the shape of the nuclear head of the sperm. Plenty of other birds, such as owls, doves, and some hummingbirds, sing persistently and repetitively. And some nonsongbirds make "instrumental" music: tail-quivering hummingbirds and wing-quivering snipe, beak-drumming woodpeckers and wing-drumming Ruffed Grouse, for example. Some "songbirds," such as the jays and crows, rarely sing but rather converse and carouse. Of course, to say that many birds don't sing is no more to cast an aspersion on them than to observe that we ourselves mostly talk and rarely sing. Like us, birds have a rich vocal language of tuneless phrases. Among both birds and people, calls, not songs, are what we hear from all but the most aroused individuals.

Permit me now another aside, this one bibliographic. A few years ago Ronald Orenstein wrote a superb book about songbirds (aptly titled *Songbirds*) that presents the whole tribe and its evolutionary neighbors and goes on to review their biology. Three recent books on birdsong also merit close attention. In *Why Birds Sing*, the musician and philosopher David Rothenberg probes the intricacies of describing (let alone explaining) birdsong and the elusiveness of musical beauty. Donald Kroodsma's long-awaited *The Singing Life of Birds* surveys "avian bioacoustics" by recounting his own "personal journeys . . . in [his] quest to understand the singing bird." He writes with the hope that "these stories and their sounds will reveal how to listen, the meaning of the music, and why we should care." And in *Birdsong*, the science writer Don Stap, accompanying Kroodsma and his colleagues on research forays, introduces general readers both to bioacoustics and to how naturalists work. Lengthy as my remarks on listening are, in some ways they merely point toward the ideas and insights to be found in these books and the earlier ones I have mentioned. Birder, read on!

To identify a singer, one must focus not just on its song's melody but also on its quality. I listen not just to the song but also to how the song is sung—to its tone of voice. A simple trill, yes, but is it dry (like a Chipping Sparrow) or rich (like a Dark-eyed Junco)? Is it fast or slow? Is it sung alone or with other notes in tow? An intricate melody, yes, but what are its syllables and phrases, and how pure or burry are its notes?

"Listen to how the song is sung." Another nascent maxim. This is how we recognize sounds all around us, by making fine distinctions regardless of the tune. That's an oboe, that's a clarinet, that's my friend's voice, this one's a Warbling Vireo, but that one's a Red-eyed Vireo; this is a Mallard but that is a Gadwall. We do the same thing with voices overheard in a marketplace. That's Japanese; there's some French; this is Spanish, but that's Italian; I think I hear some German, Hebrew, Urdu, Swahili, Russian . . . What the speakers are saying may be incomprehensible, but we can tell the languages themselves apart by their cadences, by their accents and stresses, their inflections, and by their tones of voice. The same with birds. But the first hours are discouraging! So many voices, so little recognition! And how exhausting it is to listen so hard! It demands a new kind of stamina. Eventually, though, by listening closely and patiently and often enough, we get to recognize the instrument, the language, the bird. In a familiar region, a varsity birder can aim to recognize every bird's song and virtually every bird's call.

Sounds can fool us, just as sights can. Usually this happens through our own inexperience, not a bird's deception, and usually we hear something slightly "off" that flags trouble. The jay's all-but-convincing imitation of a hawk lacks a certain throatiness. The distant grosbeak's song reminds us of a robin in a hurry—but with its slurs and quavers, a drunken one. Aside from famous mimic species like mockingbirds, the individual copycat is exceptionally rare. (And those mockers give themselves away by their very bravura in imitating so many other species all at once.) Even so, sham happens and we can fall for it—a Blue-winged Warbler sings a Golden-winged song, for example. And occasionally the song can astonish: one message to BirdChat reported a Rufous-sided Towhee, scarcely an imitator, that sang "a perfect White-eyed Vireo song." It need not even be a bird: in central California, Merriam's Chipmunk can sound uncannily like a Northern Pygmy-Owl. Once, when I thought I had called in this cryptic owl for a very skilled British visitor, I whispered, "It's in that tree twenty feet away." "Yes," my friend murmured. "I can see it shaking its bushy tail."

Listen to how the song is sung.

Now and then I encounter an odd situation. Birders sometimes cannot hear a slight, high-pitched sound I am trying to point out when I imitate it at one pitch, but they pick it up when I imitate it at a pitch closer to the real thing. Then, once they hear the sound, they detect it again clearly. We have to listen at the right pitch, to be aurally "in focus." Otherwise we may miss a sound, especially a high-pitched one, that our ears have picked up but our brain has not registered. As we age (at least we males), we may lose much of our ability to hear very high pitches. But I think we get less adept, too, at *focusing* on high pitches that, in fact, we still do hear. We hear but we fail to notice. The birdsong identification expert Ernie Jardine has suggested calling this having a "lazy ear," the aural counterpart of a lazy, unfocused eye.

With hearing much more than with seeing, a prolonged effort may put us in a numbed state of overload, when bird sounds blend into a kind of aural surf. Our ears continue to take them in, but our brain tunes them out. Long days struggling with a foreign language have this same effect; exhausted, we spend evenings bathing in sounds largely devoid of meaning. We have run through our aural stamina. Tomorrow we will be fresh to hear more French—or birds.

Tapes and CDs of bird sounds are powerful learning aids, especially before a trip to distant places and unfamiliar species. But how can we learn to listen at all? For songs, I recommend Ernie Jardine's little book, *Bird Song Identification Made Easy*. He organizes songs by their elements and does it so well that birders anywhere can keep adding, on their own, more species to his roster of eastern North American ones. My copy of his book is filling up with notes about western species. And staring at pictures of birds as you listen to recordings of them singing can work instructive magic. Rote learning? You bet!

Learning bird sounds from recordings is like learning a language from a dictionary.

Most recordings overwhelm the listener with all their species. They do not teach how to listen. The sound snippets go by too quickly, and they are rarely arranged by types of song or call. Learning from these resources is like learning a language from a dictionary—a glum prospect. Instead, for birders seeking audio help, I think Richard Walton and Robert Lawson's several *Birding by Ear* tapes or CDs are the best choice. Even more than Jardine, these authors have grouped birds by the kinds of songs they sing. birds that say their names, whistlers, trillers, high-pitched singers, and so on. After listening to a few repetitions, one's ear becomes attuned to song types, to how the song is sung, so that songs heard in the field seem to fall naturally into one or another generic type. The situation begins to feel manageable. Confidence gathers; comprehension follows.

But learning to recognize birds with our ears is too subtle a skill to leave to audio shortcuts. Eventually, we must gain it in the field, with mentors: birders, standing still, whispering to each other, "Listen . . . There it goes again."

"Listen. There it goes again."

We know what we hear, but what do birds hear? The range of a songbird's voice coincides with ours enough to say that, extremes and oddities aside, we probably hear a lot of each other. Of course, songbirds are mostly tiny compared to us, and commensurately high-pitched. Like Gulliver in his travels, we hear most songbirds' voices as the high-pitched twittering of Lilliputians, and they probably hear ours as the rumblings of Brobdingnagians.

When it comes to the pace of their singing, though, songbirds leave us behind. We are too slow to catch how they shape their songs. Their slurs and trills and twitters combine so quickly, we miss what is going on inside them. But the birds don't; they separate sounds far faster than we can. We have to slow the pace and even lower the pitch in order to enter many birds' songs on our own, more lumbering terms. (Depending on one's computer software and Internet connection, sound-slowing and pitch-lowering programs like the scientists' Canary or Raven or the musicians' less pricey Transcribe! now make this possible.) Then . . . surprise! The Winter Wren sounds like a celestial thrasher; the House Finch's burry sigh turns out to have immense complexity; the Hermit Thrush's phrase-ending buzz is the very stuff of music; the Yellowthroat sings not "witchity witchity" but intricate syllables full of internal sounds and inflections that vary bird by bird. No wonder birds can tell each other apart individually by their songs and calls; they are full of variations and idiosyncrasies that we miss but they hear.

When birds sing or call, what in fact are they saying or at least sharing? As have many others, I have already opined that songs are about sex and real estate and that calls are mostly interjections and commands. Charles Hartshorne took into account the altogether other possibility that, in part, songs express birds' pleasure. That is, many birds may sing because it feels good. Hartshorne argued that any elaborate and manifestly skilled behavior indulged in as widely and persistently as birdsong is, and even at the risk of attracting predators, must given some sort of pleasure to the actors; otherwise, why would they persist, especially in apparently unnecessary quantities and situations? The pleasure need not be of the self-conscious, aesthetic sort that we ourselves experience upon hearing birds sing; it could well be one of relief—the pleasure of a quenched thirst. Of course, plenty of rapt listeners (recently Alan Powers, for example) have written in this vein, but more "impressionistically."

Back in "Watching Gulls and Doing Science," I asked if ascribing a human psychic state like pleasure to birds doesn't

Elaborate, skillful behavior indulged in persistently must give the actor pleasure.

violate a taboo against projecting human qualities onto other animals—that is, a taboo against anthropomorphism. The great naturalist Alexander Skutch is my guide on this treacherous ground. He points out that we accept easily enough that birds and people have comparable structural characters, for example, that a bird's wing is built like our arm. In fact, resemblances like those provide some of our standard evidence of evolutionary relatedness. Yet we run into trouble whenever we propose that, when people and birds behave alike, they have comparable feelings and emotions. As Skutch says, "... consciousness is always an inference, never a datum."

But Skutch then puts the conundrum in these compelling terms:

> Our imagination is limited by our experience. It is difficult for us to imagine any feelings, affections, or

enjoyments that might give value to another creature's life wholly different from those that have enhanced our own. . . . Among the experiences that might enrich the life of . . . many birds and mammals, are pleasure in spontaneous activity, such as flying and soaring by birds, gamboling by quadrupeds, swimming by dolphins; the comfort of companionship in a perilous world; affection for mates, especially among animals continuously paired; emotional attachment to nests and dependent young; aesthetic response to beautiful colors and melodious sounds; a bird's delight in its own singing. . . .

We cannot prove that nonhuman animals enjoy living, are emotionally attached to mates and young, or are attracted to beauty. . . . But instead of stigmatizing the attempt to demonstrate humanlike psychic qualities in animals, we should welcome every indication of their presence. . . . The probability that they occur should raise our estimate of the worth of animate life, making us feel less alone in a world overcrowded with other organisms.

Here is a case in point: one aspect of birdsong that birdwatchers rather neglect is the quiet, almost murmured, singing that many birds engage in together around the nest or alone in tranquil circumstances. Romantics call it "whisper singing"; harder-nosed types call it "sub-singing." It may involve all sorts of compulsions, stimuli, and motives. Sometimes male birds in their first spring, still learning to sing full songs, sing softly as if to practice what they have heard from adults and will soon master. But sometimes the situation is more intriguing. Barry MacKay has written this about the murmurings of a far-from-home Painted Redstart he nurtured through a Canadian winter:

> The subsong was invariably sung only when the bird appeared to be completely content. He would fluff the feathers of his flanks, and either perched on one foot or sitting flat, he quietly sang. His eyes seemed to be partly shut, and his head was very slightly tilted back. His throat would puff in and out, and sometimes he'd look around as he sang. This whisper singing would happen only when all was calm and quiet. He did not mind familiar humans in the room so long as we were not moving about. He did not mind sound so long as it was a monotonous and familiar background sound . . . Any change or disturbance would cause him to become instantly alert. Otherwise, when he was finished with his subsong, or during a pause, he would often stretch high on both legs or spread his wings, much like a human rousing from a brief bit of daydreaming. Then, perhaps, he would fly over to take nourishment or water from small dishes we provided . . . or return to his subsong.

Around the nest, a birder can often hear parents warbling softly to each other, and sometimes those that are brooding will sing quietly to themselves. Our first impulse is to infer moments of contentment or perhaps affection, or at least of relaxation, as with MacKay's redstart. But Rosemary Jellis, who for many years observed and even raised songbirds in her house and garden in England, noticed that during some nesting and courtship ceremonies that included what she called quiet warblings and twitterings, "the excited state of the bird is revealed in movement: a shivering of the wings too rapid to be called fluttering." We birders often see silent fledglings shiver their wings this way when they are being fed by parents.

She reported, too, that many tinkling sounds—treble piano passages, even frying bacon—could send the young birds into "a state of wing-shivering excitement" and set them to softly warbling. On a more amateurish note, a jay I have taught to take peanuts from my hand mutters softly but constantly as it sits nearby and ponders the risk. No shivering here; maybe that jay is swearing under its breath. Whatever its meaning, whispered song is invariably striking, even enchanting, as if the bird were confiding. Listen closely and patiently; you will hear it with new ears.

Finally, when it comes to birdsong, what about ourselves as we listen? Why do I so often feel a little thrill when I hear a bird sing? My reaction seems to me to be so thorough, to lie so deep in my flesh, that I think it must have an immense biological antiquity. Alexander Skutch remarks on our human loneliness in nature. When we hear a bird sing, I believe we feel, for that instant, somehow less alone.

PISHING

One of the strangest things beginning birders encounter is "pishing," the weird noises birders make when we seek to lure little birds from cover. Hunters use expensive horns: crow calls and duck calls, turkey calls, deer calls, even wounded-rabbit calls. They even have national competitions! Birders just pish.

Pishing takes several voices. Some birders make a squeaky kissing noise with the back of their hand or a couple of fingers, and they may throw in a few squishy sounds with puckered lips. Some dentally gifted birders can make faint high-pitched whistles by pushing or sucking air between their front teeth. Some use their tongue and lips to produce a high, sibilant *psz-psz-psz*, rather like a hoarse Brown Creeper, or a more defined *pssp-pssp*, or an airy sound like *ss-wss-wss*. These basics lead to innumerable and sometimes bizarre personal variations.

Quiet and intermittent imitations of a small owl also bring out birds to mob the ersatz predator. Although they look like key-ring charms, the fabled Audubon Bird Calls work, too, after a fashion—something to do with fidgety hands—but too often they sound like the very high, thin alarm calls that birds utter when an accipiter is near, and so they quiet the scene rather than enliven it. With practice (and a little powdered rosin), the Audubon gadget can imitate a great range of bird sounds, but with practice so can a birder by pishing.

Pishing is not even a pale shadow of luring with tapes or CDs. Even so, I urge restraint around nesting birds. If you know they are there, just wait patiently for them to show themselves. They will, and while you wait, you will see far more than you would by any pish-and-go routine.

As far as I can tell, pishing is a thoroughly North American practice. The Europeans I have birded with search silently and observe me pishing with polite amusement. They seem to find as many birds as I do. I have tried pishing songbirds in France and Italy, and with some species it almost seems to work. But songbirds there face firing lines that North American ones cannot imagine. And so those European birds, when they spot me, drop like stones, doubtless with visions of blackbird pie or ortolan tart in their little heads.

In North America, pishing does seem to attract birds now and then, despite the jokes about its random effects. Very responsive birds include chickadees and titmice and others of that tiny tribe, and their antics bring in other birds. In hedgerows, some sparrow species are famously responsive, again raising shyer species. But even the most beguiling noises will not work on birds that couldn't care less — for example, exhausted migrants cowering in the bushes on the Dry Tortugas. And there seems to be a seasonal or at least a circumstantial element to effective pishing: sibilant noises work well with winter songster flocks, distressed-young cries alert parents in the summer, and alarm calls at any season raise many sparrows for a moment from dense thickets. Some birders resort to sudden, very loud pishing, at which an entire hedge's crowd of birds may leap into the open, then just as quickly drop back into cover, I think thoroughly alarmed. That was your chance! Even a responsive bird, once it has shown some curiosity about your funny noises, rarely falls for the same ruse again right away. It quickly sees the game for what it is, and probably connects you with it. So be prepared, when you pish, to note a raised bird's traits at first sight. After that comes the waiting game.

First, let the habitat settle down.

Some of pishing's unpredictability may reflect poor technique. First let the habitat settle down, get out of the middle of the trail and into a little cover, and do not move at all or talk *at all*. To pish and walk at the same time is a clever but useless skill. When pishing, do not stare at your quarry. *Never point straight-armed* at the raised bird—a sure way to send it scurrying. And stop quickly to let any agitated birds take over the chore; they will raise a better fuss than you can. Major leaguers I have observed pish very sparingly, if at all, just enough to engage birds' curiosity. Then they stand still and look and listen. Making too many funny noises can advertise our presence and so work against effective searching. As someone on BirdChat once suggested, birds may well conclude that pishing is merely another strange thing that people do: "People? They hiss."

A few birders I have spent field days with seem to be able to bring birds down from the sky itself by pishing. I wonder if they are making noises birds hear but none of the rest of us do. And I have met a couple of birders who did not pish so much as whistle, tongue in teeth, imitating very high-pitched, complex birdsong. Some birders can whistle with an apparent veracity that is truly astonishing. Christopher Wood of Connecticut can whistle complex, high-pitched birdsong with uncanny deftness, and so could the legendary California ornithologist Luis Baptista, famous for his bird song studies. He seemed able to *charm* birds to him.

Recalling Luis Baptista's charm, maybe I should correct myself: I said that European birders do not pish and that birds there do not respond well to this lure. But maybe I spoke too quickly. If when in Italy, you visit the great basilica at Assisi, look at Giotto's thirteenth-century fresco of Saint Francis preaching to the birds. His lips are puckered. The birds gathered at his feet listen attentively. He is pishing.

LURING WITH TAPES AND CDS

Short of shooting them, as birders once did, we probably disturb breeding birds most when we lure them into view by playing recordings of their songs or calls. It is no wonder that birders' feelings about this practice run strong.

Pishing intrudes into birds' lives, but tapes and CDs do so enormously more.

Birds, intensely social creatures, spend a lot of their waking hours responding to others of their kind. In fact, the hard-wired readiness of birds' responses is why birders use recordings as lures at all. Someone that imitates a bird's rival or friend imitates a common figure in that bird's life. But a taped song may interfere with a bird's egg-brooding or nestling-feeding chores. The last thing a breeding bird needs is an intruding rival. Especially during their weeks of defending a territory and claiming a mate, many birds, hormonally sensitized, react very strongly to songs suddenly played in their midst. At those times they show all the upset that we would show upon hearing an intruder in our home. Think of the adrenaline rush even the illusion of a prowler's nighttime shadow can bring! Breeding birds may respond to recordings with every sign that they, too, are having adrenaline rushes: frenzied sounds and apoplectic hopping about. These are not times for philosophical debates about anthropomorphism. These are times to back off.

Even more alarming, some species are famously intolerant of *any* human disturbance when they are nesting. Responsible birders stay away altogether. Around nesting Northern Goshawks, for instance, only foolhardy birders (yes, I among them) venture at all. Even if we may doubt stories that a few skittish species abandon their eggs upon the very sight of us, we properly leave them entirely alone around their nests. Extending this caution and consideration, why not just let *all* birds nest in at least tape-free peace?

Another circumstance that ought to persuade the conscientious birder to forgo recordings is the presence of many other birders at a site. So many of us converge on the famous hot spots—the meccas of the birding world—that, even as it is, we continually risk bothering the birds there just by walking about. Tapes and CDs would only make matters worse, so they are forbidden. National parks ban them, too, and so do many other natural preserves, public and private, hot spot or not. I have visited some of these places with major-league birders, and, silently, we have always found our target species. Perhaps the searches have taken longer and tested our skills, but they have been all the more engrossing. We have looked and listened all the more assiduously, and this has enriched the entire experience. Too often the tape, or even pishing, expresses merely the birder's impatience.

But there are some other circumstances that would seem to permit or even favor the restrained use of recordings to lure especially stealthy birds into a vocal or visible response. Out of nesting time, birds' reactions to tapes often seem more puzzled and inquisitive than challenging. In the chaparral along the West Coast, for example, Wrentits habitually sing from the very depths of thickets and sometimes will not budge; hearing a tape, one may hop up and look about before going back into cover. Did this lure reward the birder's impatience, or did it avoid an hour's forlorn and intrusive pishing? Responding to the tape may have put the Wrentit at increased risk of predation, but so can our lingering and poking about. This is especially so when a whole group of birders seeks a bird. One person, still and silent, may soon enough blend into the habitat, so that birds there more or less resume their interrupted activities. But a group of people milling about (and that is what groups of birders cannot help but do) is another matter. That Wrentit, say, or a rail that has retreated into the reeds, may be as distracted in its hiding place as the one that has emerged briefly to check out a luring song.

It may come to a choice of intrusions.

So it may often come down to a choice of intrusions. The alternative to disturbing birds at all must be not to seek certain species at all. I doubt that avian feelings always exist at fever pitch; I believe most non-nesting birds will tolerate our restrained curiosity. But I stress the element of restraint. A bird's response gained, its song or call heard or the bird seen, a birder should not continue to lure it. To do so is sheer annoyance, tantamount to poking at the animal in its behavioral cage. If a group even without tapes loiters in some bird's habitat once that bird has shown itself, that, too, gratuitously annoys. While field ornithologists have their special needs and ways of prolonging their observations, satisfied twitchers should quit a shy bird's vicinity with thoughtful dispatch. It is a way of saying thank you to the bird that has cooperated with us in an altogether one-way give-and-take: the bird gave, we took.

STALKING

At all levels of expertise, most birding is a stroll. When I come home from a day of birding, my wife, Louise, often laughs: "I hope you don't think you got real exercise." Sometimes we birders may plunge into thickets, but rarely for long or far, and once we are in them we generally stand still. Only a few of us traverse the forest or penetrate the swamp. We tend to stay on trails. We have our reasons: trails have better sight lines than dense woods, and swamps impede. When we do strike out from the path, our inexpert forays often frighten off the birds we seek. And in parks and reserves, getting off the path can bring down tiresome scoldings about what would happen if everyone did it (but of course, that's just the point: hardly anyone does do it).

Sometimes, though, the view from the path is not enough; we want to stalk our bird. Ocean beaches and lake shores and open fields may demand it as a matter of course. Bear in mind that when ornithologists of an earlier age collected small birds, they had to get very close to their quarry to shoot them with dust shot. They did not just blow the birds out of the sky the way grouse hunters do in the movies. This sort of close approach to birds is still entirely feasible, as today's fewer but equally skillful collectors know. And collectors' stalking skills will work today, too, for birders who want simply to observe birds close up.

At the start, a caveat: A close, off-trail approach may well disturb the bird. Close approaches *to* the bird when we are stalking are like close approaches *by* the bird when we are luring with tapes, with the added effects of the stalker's body actually invading the bird's habitat. Both modes of contact require discretion. "But I mean no harm" scarcely reassures the bird or erases the footprints. As with tapes, so with stalking: When what seems like an upset bird says, "Go away!" I go away.

Three factors converge in stalking. One is *staring eyes.* Musicians, actors, politicians, and teachers have to expect the stares of strangers; some even enjoy them. But most of us North Americans find being stared at disconcerting. Staring (like blatant pointing) invades our privacy. Many birds, too, seem to be upset by staring, probably because most of the stares they get come from predators.

If you can, hide your eyes. Writing in *The Horned Lark*, Byron Butler advises wearing a baseball cap: "The bird on a branch looking back at you is looking at your eyes to see what you are up to. . . . The bill of a baseball cap provides a shield (an ultra-mini blind) by which I can hide my eyes and break up the outline of my face. I frequently turn my head and body away, looking off to the side of the bird, then peek

When the bird says, "Go away."

under my cap in a Princess Di fashion to sneak a view." We practice discreet eyeing in elevators and other awkward social milieus; we know how to do it with other people. Switch the knack to watching birds.

The hugest stare of all is our binoculars'. Their front (objective) lenses each measure more than an inch across. A dozen birders with their binoculars challenge a bird with two dozen giant eyes, like a little troupe just arrived from another planet. No wonder the bird edges around to the far side of the branch.

A second factor in stalking is *body language.* Even though we have a rich verbal language, we constantly if unconsciously read each other for nonverbal messages, and we broadcast postural messages unwittingly as well as on

Peek from under your cap, Princess Di fashion.

purpose. Edward T. Hall called this our "silent language." Birds, too, read each others' bodies for postural and kinetic messages about intentions. We human beings miss most of their signals. But birds read *us*. They size us up. Our challenge when stalking is to reduce what evidently comes across to most birds as our menacing body language. For example, birds seem to take alarm at symmetry: frontal views, stereo eyes. That is the posture from which most predators' attacks begin. We can avoid this symmetry when approaching birds by using zigzag, oblique routes, and by presenting side views of ourselves.

Anything that reduces our tall stature also helps in stalking small birds. To little songsters, we are perfectly enormous. Consider a sparrow that stands three inches tall on the ground. A person between five feet tall and six-foot-three is twenty to twenty-five times that sparrow's height. A creature comparably taller than we are would loom beside us 100 to 150 feet high: ten to fifteen stories tall! Imagine that; it will make you try to lower yourself when stalking little birds. Especially in the open, a little folding stool will do this. Sit as much as you can, and when you move a little closer to the bird, rise from the stool *slowly* and facing sideways. Even kneel or squat. Birds may think you are mad, but they won't think you are about to lunge. They may even watch, fascinated. One fact persists through all your stalking: the birds know you are there.

Slowness is an essential element of stalking: patience and deliberation, long moments of inaction as birds accustom themselves afresh to your somewhat altered position while you look away, an ambulatory tai chi. If the best stalk is motionless, the next best has the least motion. On a beach, meander well to one side of the gulls. Let them get used to you over and over. Stop and scope something else—or pretend to. Look away a lot. Project a distinct lack of interest in those birds, even if you are churning inside with the growing conviction that one of them is an Ivory Gull.

As stalking succeeds, a third factor emerges: *critical distance*. We can feel its play in our own lives when, for example, people of some other culture position themselves at their comfortable conversational distance but we North

Americans feel they are too close. (Again see E. T. Hall, this time *The Hidden Dimension*.) To us, critical distance is a convention, but think at what cost birds have learned to keep critical distances from predators, which birds understandably may take stalking birders to be. Alan Powers says, "For most [songbirds], twenty or thirty feet is roughly equivalent to a yard among humans. Closer than that, and you are up-close-and-personal, within the bird's urge-to-flee space." When a bird flies away, he suggests, "We were in his space before he was in ours."

As the distance between you and your bird narrows, be alert for its "intention movements," the craned neck, the widened eyes, the raised crown, the slight shifts and crouches that precede its taking flight—more body language. These signs tell you to stop, relax, look away, wait awhile. Byron Butler put it this way: "Too many birders see intention movements, then think they have to get a good look before the bird is gone. They don't realize that in doing so they are actually pushing the bird to fly. Learn to be patient." Finally, the bird says, "No closer." It is a palpable moment. Accept it, maybe with a slow drift to the side for better light, and make the best of it from there.

Getting very close to a wild bird takes real skill. One must observe its intention movements unobtrusively but with great care, sensitive to initially unfamiliar clues about curiosity or anxiety. At first, misunderstandings are bound to botch the stalk. The absorption I feel as I stalk must complement the bird's own as we observe each other.

Finally, the bird says,
"No closer."

And stalking includes eventually leaving the bird in peace; it is not just a matter of sidling up but also one of backing off thoughtfully and easing away. Successful stalk or not, I find that the thrills of mutual attention—the bird's and mine together as the distance between us closes, and then the relaxation as we part—are among the reasons I go birding.

Besides these three tactics, of course many others come into play when stalking. My boyhood hero, the intrepid naturalist William Beebe, once compiled a dozen of them for observing birds in the tropical rain forest. Here are some of those that apply, too, to our tamer efforts:

- "When a wild creature is near, keep eyes partly closed" to reduce the effect of staring.

- "When listening to faint sounds, keep mouth slightly open (as lovers of music do in the top gallery of the opera)."

- In the woods, "move only when the wind blows and moves the leaves."

- "When approaching a singing bird, take a step during each song; many birds will not notice."

- Try not to cough or clear your throat loudly. And talk, if you must, in a low voice but never in "a hissing whisper."

Take notes.

NOTES ABOUT RARITIES

When I go birding, if I am not working (well, "working") at some project, I rarely take notes except upon my return home, when I make a bird list for the day, add up counts if I am monitoring a patch, and record some recollections. Few birders I know do more than this. But one situation that converts my carefree ways on the spot into investigative reporting is encountering a rare bird. Then the pencil and paper (three by five-inch index cards) come out, and I start taking notes.

Reporters take notes. If we share our observations, we are reporters of nature, and we should take notes, too. Otherwise we will surely misquote our sources. Even if nature cannot sue us over the result, other birders can rightly doubt us, and without notes we soon enough start to doubt ourselves—an unpleasant feeling. An observation worth sharing is one worth noting. You can toss your notes away, but you cannot take trustworthy notes long after the fact. If you wait, your notes will be more about your memory than about your observation; you will be consulting your recollection and not the bird. But, you say, you can remember what you see and hear, at least until you get home and write notes there. For routine lists and simple counts, yes. But as every study of memory attests, we muddle and forget details with disconcerting speed and ease. This is especially so, and especially lamentable, when the notes would have described the details of an unfamiliar bird.

So, anticipating that I may come upon a rare bird some day and need to document the occasion, I occasionally practice by taking rare-bird notes about a familiar bird. One's first attempts at notes are to a proficient naturalist's notes what stick figures are to an artist's drawings, but they improve rapidly. Novice reporters are bound to miss what a more seasoned one would catch, but one's eyes and ears sharpen quickly with focused use. I think the only way to progress as a reporter is to take throwaway notes, poor as they are at first. Take them doggedly and in great quantity. The great golfer Bobby Jones once said, "You only learn when you lose." That goes for taking notes, too.

Notes to document sightings of rare birds are of a special sort. Birders end up submitting them as evidence to bird records committees. I have read some instructions about documenting rarities that seem to me so general ("look closely and record carefully"), they scarcely can help anyone who is just learning this skill. Other instructions strike me as too detailed, like a map drawn at too fine a scale. Here are some middle-level suggestions that I hope may cut through to clarity.

Read all the examples you can find of documentation of rarities. Donna Dittmann and Greg Lasley provide examples and excellent advice in their article, "How to Document Rare Birds." If you absorb the various ways bird reports have been put together, imitation will give you the beginnings of good ones of your own, and practice will give you competence in this little genre. Mastering bird reports can feel like learning some obscure dialect. But if you find a rarity, it will suddenly be the dialect you need to speak, and speak accurately.

Learn to draw ten-second sketches of the major bird types—connected ovals, if nothing more—and make yourself

Trace, imitate, repeat.

practice one-minute sketches of real birds. Recording the traits of a bird by annotating even the most rudimentary drawing is much easier than enumerating them on blank paper with no such map to guide the inventory. I start my notes by making a quick outline sketch (not of the bird itself but simply of its general body type); then I write. Drawing little lines to connect the central sketch to my verbal commentary keeps me aware of what parts of the bird I have dealt with, what I have neglected, what traits merit special comment and satellite drawings, and what parts I need to look at again before the bird flies or (almost as quickly) my memory fades.

Mike Patterson's "How to Write Convincing Details" can help you with your very first bird outlines. As I write this in 2005, his instructions are at www.pacifier.com/ ~mpatters/details/details.html. He provides a clever trio of sketches in the making. They transform themselves from ovals to finished pieces before your very eyes and ought to embolden even the shyest among us to add simple graphics to our kit of manual skills. Taking a few minutes to learn this basic dexterity is no harder than learning to shape a few new cursive letters. And David Sibley's *Birding Basics* has a dozen superb drawings of bird body types: gull, duck, hawk, tall wader, shorebird, songbird, and others. By enlarging them on a photocopier and then repeatedly tracing them, you will find that drawing these outlines becomes habitual even if still very rough. And with just this little effort, *provided you keep practicing*, you will gain a reporting skill you can use for the rest of your life: "Here, I'll draw you what I mean."

Learn to draw one-minute sketches.

As you practice faithfully (just a few drawings a week), the habit matures; and your sketching takes on a certain confidence. Then making graphic notes will reward you with an added benefit. Looking and drawing will cross-examine each other. As I draw, I realize that I have looked insufficiently. As I look, I realize I have drawn inaccurately, usually by drawing what I assume, not what I see. I have put a slightly wrong-shaped beak on the bird, or the wing bar I put in isn't quite there. In written notes we can hide behind words' ambiguities, but we cannot hide behind our drawings. Wordless, they speak all too directly; at least they do when drawn by artless hands.

Annotating a drawing teaches terminology and how to use it clearly. I keep a few fully labeled drawings of bird body types (now ones from Sibley's *Birding Basics*) in the back of my field guide. That way, I can use them as crib cards to remember the features I should include in my notes. The major leaguers do it by heart, but the rest of us need a little help. *The Basics of Bird Identification: Bird Topography*, a little book from the Canadian periodical *Birders Journal*, also illustrates the parts of birds. It is adapted from the British booklet *The New Approach to Identification*, by Grant and Mullarney. The names of birds' feather groups and structural parts ought to be (let's hope unaffectedly) part of every varsity birder's vocabulary. That way, they become home addresses for traits.

The bird's behavior belongs in any documentation too, even if the bird does "nothing." Gait, wing beat, tail-twitching, postures, feeding behavior, flocking or its absence, kinglet-like edginess or vireo-like lethargy, interspecific interactions—the more you watch, the more you see, the more you report in your notes. And do not neglect bird sounds. The merest pips and peeps are vocal traits, often as telling as visual ones. Finally, take ecological notes: not only about the overall kind of place you found the bird but also about the bird's most immediate habitat. *Where* in the tree? *Where* on the beach or mudflat? The bird has come to this place, even if it was forced to, and has chosen a little part of it. Its precise choice is as revealing as the intimate surroundings of our own lives.

Photographs can never replace the observation-directing efforts of taking manual notes, but bird records committees nowadays often demand them. Fair enough, but how to get them? Long lenses often capture birds as mere specks; spotting scopes, though cumbersome, provide much bigger images—maybe not pictures for the ages, but good enough to document sightings. Just focus the scope and aim the camera through it. With auto-exposure, a single-lens reflex or a digital camera can make this exercise simplicity itself. Even using a cheap point-and-shoot camera on your scope may turn out well, if you aim and pray—and practice ahead.

Take too many notes. If you do not, you will discover to your dismay that, in your excitement and your unfamiliarity with the rare bird, you skipped a key trait and need to go back. But the gods, amused, will not let you see this bird again.

We tally numbers as well as species.

COUNTING SWIFTLY

On various bird clubs' annual Christmas Bird Counts, we tally numbers as well as species; counting is easy to do on every birding day. Rather than keep a laborious running list, I reckon the day's birds numerically at midday and again at day's end. With practice, this sort of cumulative recollection can provide an effortless census even of abundant species. The estimates are personally consistent, even if chronically a little too high or too low; less numerous birds get more precise counts. Variables like routes and weather roughen the results, but keeping track of quantities this way lets even a casual birder monitor the rise and fall of local populations.

Over the decades, counting keeps a check on memories, too. If I recall how shorebirds once covered the Monomoy sand flats and ducks filled the Central Valley sky, do my notes say so? If a few decades ago Mourning Doves were thought to be going the way of the Passenger Pigeon, do my recorded counts bear out this now unbelievable concern? Barn Owls were once common in the Midwest—or were they? When did seeing a European Starling along the Pacific coast last merit telling other birders, the way seeing a Eurasian Collared-Dove there does now? Did Brown Pelicans ever get as scarce as I seem to remember? Are Brown-headed Cowbirds really that much more common around here this summer than last? These sorts of questions call for tallies.

There are lots of shrewd techniques for counting birds. But sometimes birds come all at once in quantities that seem to overwhelm. Blackbirds pour from their roost. Ducks crowd a lake and gulls cover a dump. Sparrows swarm near the ground or warblers cascade through the trees. Buteos by the score or even by the hundred rise into the sky. Birds can occur in flocks too big for one-by-one counting or reasonably accurate after-hours guessing, confronting us with problems of on-the-spot estimation. How can we record more than "scads"?

Birds of a feather often do flock together, sometimes by family (foraging sparrows, gleaning warblers, swallows), sometimes even by species (American Robin, Sooty Shearwater, American Crow, Red-winged Blackbird, Canada Goose). Birds of a feather share needs and impulses, and they apparently seek each other's company. Dennis Paulson has pointed out to me that aerodynamics plays a role, too: even similar species may fly in subtly different ways, as when sandpipers in flocks separate by species just before they land. So our challenge as birders is usually to estimate numbers of like things.

Most of us have an intuitive grasp of five objects, probably thanks to our five-fingered hands. Some of us take in six or seven or even a few more similar items at a glance. All of us can enlarge our numerical grasp, but probably not by much. Try estimating, instead of counting, little groups of things. Any objects will do. How many books in that row or windows in that wall? How many people on that street corner? How many cyclists in that line? How many cars in that lot? Estimate birds whenever you see a flock. But rather than taking on a blanket of gulls, a cloud of blackbirds, a raft of ducks, or a river of shearwaters, start with little flocks.

Most of us have an intuitive grasp of how many fingers and toes we have.

As an early exercise, try to take in five similar objects at a glance, then six at once . . . then seven . . . Try to *feel* what these quantities look like when they are not arranged into orderly patterns, like the dots on dice. Then, since we have been taught to think decimally, stare at groups of ten—ten fingers or toes for starters, then ten plates, ten books, ten people, ten gulls, ten sparrows, ten ducks. Your aim is to grasp "ten-ness": what ten actually looks like, *feels* like. The size of your objects matters, even among birds. A flock of ten sparrows feels fewer than ten flying pelicans; ten flying terns feel different from ten sitting ducks. You probably will come to ten via five-and-five, seven-and-three, or other such rapid combinations, but try to get to "gulps of ten," to make ten feel the way five does now. Counting by tens lets you count *ten times faster* than by ones. A very few wizards seem to see even fifty birds at a glance! But I think they may be combining tens or some other small units at lightning speed without even realizing it.

Meanwhile, practice with still larger quantities. To develop a numerical "feel" for bird flocks, Robert Arbib, in his article "On the Art of Estimating Numbers," has suggested counting sunflower seeds. Repeatedly toss two or three dozen seeds onto a plain tray. Stare at them for just a few seconds, too short a time to count. Force yourself to look away sharply, say their quantity aloud (to commit yourself), then actually count. These handfuls of seeds are your practice flocks of birds. Over weeks, if you have the patience to do this many, many times, you will find you get much less clumsy in combining the tens (or so) that bring you to a fast yet accurate estimate. Your eye is gaining quantitative fluency. You are counting swiftly.

When you encounter standing flocks—say, a modest-sized flock of resting gulls—exploit your luck. Stop and estimate how many birds are in the group. Stare at ten of them, then count the flock in ten- or twenty-bird gulps. Bigger flocks will force you to units of fifty or even a hundred. Quickly combine tens of gulls into a hundred, then build by hundreds until you have estimated a third or half the flock, then triple or double your tally to reckon the entire group. Then, as a check, repeat the process in the reverse direction.

One morning I did this from an overlook, estimating a flock of gulls on a beach. First, starting on the left, I took in ten gulls, then twenty. I reckoned by twenties five times: a hundred gulls. Continuing rightward, I gulped three more hundred-gull units until I got to what seemed like the flock's center: four hundred birds in the left half. It took four more hundred-bird gulps to reach the flock's right margin: eight hundred gulls altogether. Then I counted in this same way from the right: a thousand birds, a bothersome difference. Were the birds packed together unevenly? I swept again from the left, this time more carefully: ten, fifty (by tens), then a hundred, and then on through the whole flock by hundreds. This time, I got a thousand gulls. A second, equally deliberate count from the right again produced a thousand. By now, familiar with them, I felt my hundred-bird gulps were getting quite accurate. Four sweeps—about twenty minutes—gave me a reasonably confirmed estimate, and (as is often the case) more birds than I first thought. Then, rather chastened by my faulty first estimate, I quietly scanned the flock to get a better feel for what a flock of a thousand gulls standing together on the beach looks like. The next time I visited that overlook I completed an exercise of this sort in a quarter hour—eventually in ten minutes, when my gull-estimating skills were honed. So can you.

That overlook made matters easy, and the flock was quiet. From the beach itself, flocks are confusing; birds hide birds, flock density changes in uncertain ways; or birds move about, coming and going, making estimates fluid. Counting merely a hundred godwits on the beach recently almost stymied me as they rushed to and fro with the surf. Practice from easy vantage points and with calm flocks. Postpone the tougher challenges. Save virtuoso play for when you get good.

Flying flocks are much harder—everything is moving at once and the clock is running—but big birds often assume simple patterns: skeins of gulls or geese, lines of scoters or pelicans. Again, start with tens, accumulate them, and so build your estimate by counting swiftly. Initially the flock will long since have flown away while you struggle on alone for a number. Eventually you will do in seconds what first took you minutes—fluency again. For a while your estimates may be way off, especially with irregular flocks of songbirds, but soon enough you will estimate with speed and accuracy.

Flying flocks of shorebirds can pose unique problems, as they ball up and swirl about. Accumulating small quantities to reckon big ones helps, but only up to a point; things are happening fast. A balled-up flock is probably uniformly dense, so you can break the confusing swarm into quarters or thirds and multiply accordingly. Compare your in-flight estimate with what you get when the flock settles down.

When linear, trailing flocks of birds are going by for a long time—loons, scoters, shearwaters, sometimes even songbirds flying across the face of the full moon—try to estimate numbers per second or per ten or twenty seconds as the birds pass through a standard field such as the field of your binoculars or your scope or the moon's disk.

Occasionally the numbers of birds get beyond scads; they get out of hand. We are told, and I believe it, that in the very old days great flocks of big birds sometimes darkened the sun. Even nowadays, on summer afternoons, huge flocks of Sooty Shearwaters skirt the shore of California's Monterey Bay, converging each dusk off a beach just south of Santa Cruz. Ordinarily these flocks number in the tens of thousands—big enough! One day a few years ago I watched spellbound as millions of these birds approached these roosting waters. At first I had taken the flock to be a dark fog bank. Awed birders around this part of the bay spoke of several million shearwaters in the eventual congregation, but no one really quantified this astounding assembly. It was like counting smoke.

Flocks of big birds often assume simple patterns.

GEAR

Of course, you already have binoculars.

BINOCULARS

When I began birding in New Jersey in the 1940s, I fell in with the Urner Club's extraordinary birders of that era. One of the best of them used gravely wounded binoculars. He bought a pair at a pawnshop every January and finished them off during the year. I recall one year's binoculars that by Labor Day had a cracked front lens and a shifty prism. I could not see through them at all. Did he miss much? Doubtless he did, now and then. And yet I remember how, as a long Christmas Bird Count wound down in the Barnegat gloom, he picked out a Harlequin Duck beyond the surf, this time with wildly misaligned optics. ("Close an eye," he suggested.) Then, to cheers, he heaved them into the Atlantic. It was New Year's Eve, time to go back to the pawnshop.

I cannot carry that off. My binoculars are my birding eyes. And while some costly tools, like computers and cameras, will perform beyond almost any demands, not so binoculars. We habitually test them to their limits. Many binoculars are equally fine under ideal conditions (such as looking across the street from the store), but they show their differences when pressed a little: a shorebird's feathers against the beach's glare, hawks aloft, sparrows in the underbrush, treetop warblers—all in a day's birding. And the avian challenges can get very tough even under the best circumstances: scrutinizing the plumages of winter longspurs or sandpipers or young gulls. That, as I recall, was when my Urner Club mentor would cadge a look through a pal's intact binocs.

The birding equipment market is huge, so optics makers tempt us with bells and whistles as much as with real advances in "imaging." We can buy auto focus and image stabilizers and "multi-magnifications" and even integrated digital cameras. Such gizmos and widgets bode ill for the nontechie. Maybe binocs are getting like computers after all. Even without the frills—which I urge you to avoid—to choose new binoculars is to embark on a confusing trip.

Of course you already have binoculars, but maybe you seek to upgrade. When and where can you test the options? The place to do that is on bird club trips, by borrowing other birders' binocs. A quick glance is not a test; it's like merely kicking the tires. Borrow them for an hour. The lenders will be thrilled to use yours and realize how much better their own are. And try out those loaners with tough challenges— against the glare, into the shadows. Assess not just brightness and clarity and field of view, but also less obvious yet equally crucial matters: eye relief, depth of focus, close focus, how the binocs feel after a while in your hands, how comfortably your fingers work the focusing wheel. Might you even try out a friend's especially appealing binocs for all of another day? Take your time, and take more than one round to test your final candidates; you will make this decision only a few times in all your birding career. In six decades of birding I have upgraded twice.

Pete Dunne has included an invaluable chapter about buying binoculars in his recent, information-packed book, *Pete Dunne on Bird Watching*. I recommend that chapter (and the whole book) to all birders, and especially to beginners. The Internet has lots of information about binoculars, too. Sites like Better View Desired (www.betterview desired.com) and dealers like Eagle Optics (www.eagle optics.com) have helped many gear-leery birders over recent years and cleared up many puzzles and technical terms. Another immense online trove of opinion, with years of correspondence among birders, some of them wonderfully gear-obsessed, is the archives of the national birding chat group BirdChat.

Because birders do change binoculars, eventually many fine used pairs should turn up on the market—many more than seem to. To what attic or elephants' graveyard do the rest go? Sometimes the classified ads in the ABA's newsletter, *Winging It*, offer them, and at very sensible prices, and word of mouth in the more active local clubs is another good source. Also, if one of our birding companions has shown up recently with a smile and new binoculars, we can recall this when we meet people seeking used optics. Maybe one of them can borrow or buy our friend's once-treasured and still perfectly good pair. Buying used equipment is always risky, but the birding community is likely to be as fair—even solicitous—a bazaar as anyone could hope to find for top-notch "pre-owned" optics.

From time to time beginners ask veteran birders to help them buy binoculars. I think beginners should buy ones that provide a clear, sharp, bright image and have a wide field of view, yet not so fine a pair that financial guilt overwhelms birding pleasure. To me, this suggests 8X binocs for about two or three hundred dollars, bought from a birdwatchers' store whose staff knows optics. But occasionally some exceptional model for less does come along, its praises sung in birding circles. Sometimes they are not especially sturdy, and usually they are not waterproof. But if they pass the rigorous viewing tests I have mentioned, they deserve careful consideration (and, perhaps, rather careful handling). I think beginners should avoid compact binoculars. Most of them, even most high-end models, have drawbacks (such as a narrow field of view or a tiny exit pupil) that outweigh their first-blush charms. But for hiking or as a backup pair, compacts obviously have much to recommend them. Keep them in the car or a coat pocket, ready for the strokes of good luck that bless the prepared birder even on the way to work.

A few hundred dollars is a lot to invest in a new hobby. But it is a mistake for beginners to buy cheap binoculars. They are only stacking the deck against themselves when it comes to enjoying an often difficult new pursuit. Flimsy optics are to birding gear what plywood boxes are to violins. A birding store (usually not a camera store) whose staff really knows binoculars can provide good models and the guidance we all need whenever we choose among them. The novice then should *buy there* and support the store that has helped so much. So should we all, if we are lucky enough to have such a store nearby.

As you edge toward the top, toward new Leica and Zeiss and Swarovski binoculars, get ready for sticker shock! When I got there, the store owner dealt with it handily. "Still, they cost less than a matched set of golf clubs," she said. "And birders don't pay greens fees."

"Still, they cost less than a set of golf clubs . . . "

SPOTTING SCOPES

Buying a spotting scope can be as perplexing as choosing binoculars. Again, as with binocs, test your candidates *at length* on bird club trips. There is no other way to sort out the options: diameter of the front (objective) lens and hence light-gathering potential, ergonomics of the focusing knob or ring, zoom versus fixed-power eyepiece, weight over a day's long haul, lenses of special glass and design or other choices of innards, and straight versus angled viewing.

We rarely put spotting scopes to anything like the demands we make on our binoculars. Most of the time we use scopes in good light and on birds that stay put (aside from seabirds viewed from shore). We tend to scope in leisurely ways. The scope power of choice for scanning is often 20X to 30X, since the field of view is wide at such a low magnification. At 20X many even so-so scopes compare well to very good ones. Is the image bright and clear? Probably, unless the glass is inferior. For years, 20X to 30X covered the full available range of spotting scope power, and it served birders well; 30X was considered very powerful; 60X was for astronomy.

Now zoom eyepieces have long been all the rage. After using one (20X to 60X) for years with a rather big scope, I switched to a 32X eyepiece. It has extraordinarily fine clarity and an uncannily wide field. Now I use it all the time. I rarely miss "the other 28X"; I have plenty of telescopic power. Sometimes I carry the zoom eyepiece in my vest pocket, but I put it to work only when, say, some truly distant speck of a seabird has me stumped. True enough, changing eyepieces is less convenient than merely twisting a barrel to change power, but I rarely make that change. And though the quality of zoom optics is widely claimed now to match that of fixed-focus optics, every look through my 32X eyepiece convinces me to stick with it.

But distant birds tantalize, and zoom eyepieces that crank the scope up to 60X and even more now cater to these situations. With eyepieces this powerful, only a scope that gathers and transmits lots of light can provide a superior image; and so at these magnifications giant models outshine all but the best smaller ones. But we birders rarely need that kind of power, even if we like to indulge in it. And above 30X the image of any distant object often shimmers wildly in the air's convection, mocking our optical strength. Soberly consider what you are going to use your scope for 95 percent of the time, and buy what you need, not what you covet. You can always trade up to that.

I recommend choosing a scope with lenses of the very best glass and optical design ("fluorite," "ED" or "HD," "apo," and other such terms). It is a pricey option, but the difference in image from what "ordinary" glass or design provides can be striking. These special glasses and designs really do provide better trueness of colors and clarity of image, hence greater ease and efficiency of use whenever conditions or the birds get challenging. And if you wear glasses, be sure to choose an eyepiece with plenty of "eye relief," which is the distance between the eyepiece surface and where your eye picks up the optimal image. In my experience, these seemingly peripheral matters—type of glass, eye relief, and so on—invariably affect the pleasure of using one's scope at all.

My spotting scope has a "straight" design: I look straight toward the object I am viewing. Many birders prefer angled viewing: they bow and look somewhat down instead of straight ahead. Angled viewing might seem awkward, but it is easy to get used to. The angled design lets tall and short people share a scope without crouching or getting on tiptoe. When I lower my tripod to let some shorter person use the scope, I always lose the bird. And an angled scope can be set on a lower, hence more stable, tripod. Were I buying a scope now, I probably would get an angled one, because I share it so much. Maybe I stick with the straight design, as I do with a fixed-focus eyepiece, out of ornery habit.

A strong scope on a weak tripod is a self-defeating combination. If one's scope is at all big, it needs a very sturdy tripod so it does not quiver in the slightest wind. If you think you will take long walks with this rig, go to the gym to build up your shoulders, if it comes to that; or put a thickly folded old towel under the tripod when you heft it or neoprene pipe-insulating tubing around its legs. Carbon fiber tripods, light and amazingly sturdy, are getting less insanely costly now, and this promises some relief. In any case, why haul any scope at all if it will deliver only a palsied image? Better, if it comes to that, to emulate my mentor of long ago with his awful binoculars and just look through your friend's.

But how much to spend on the best scope optics?

MONOPODS

When, for some reason, I cannot bring along a tripod for scoping, I have found that using a small (but not teeny) scope at 20X or even 30X on a monopod works surprisingly well. A monopod is more portable than a tripod. If portability is not a problem, then by all means use a tripod for its stability and for the physical independence it gives you from your scope. (For example, you can stand back and share a view.)

A monopod can greatly enhance some binocular birding, too. Some people rest their binocs on a hiker's staff, but I like my monopod's precise vertical adjustability; I have added a homemade T-bar, as I explain below, to suit it for binocs. Compared to free-hand use, a monopod's support provides such steadiness that my 8X binocs feel almost as if they had doubled their power. You may think your hands are rock steady, but they aren't. Try reading distant text or looking at a star with and without support; you will find that hand-held binocs are constantly moving, jiggling the image, even at 8X. Good photographers using long lenses rely on at least a monopod to steady their rigs; take their hint.

Another advantage of monopod-supported binoculars is that they do not weary the arms and shoulders, so objects can be examined at great length; in effect, you can scope with them. I use a monopod to scan pond borders for rails and mudflats for shorebirds, reveling in an immense field of view, outstanding image, and fine maneuverability. On study days (see page 43), a monopod lets me examine individual birds without interruption. And on a recent trip to the Rockies, I used my monopod dawn after dawn to survey the tundra for hours in search of the legendary White-tailed Ptarmigan. The binocular image of the tundra was as steady as a diorama; every moving creature (but no ptarmigan) jumped out.

By setting the monopod to somewhat more than eye height, I can slant it a little for comfort and sort of lean into it. With a spotting scope, a tilt head lets me move a scope through moderate vertical adjustments. With binoculars, I can aim even fairly high into trees by rolling them on my monopod's homemade T-bar. I hold on mostly to the scope or the binoculars, not the monopod itself, and relax my weight onto the rig; stability with a monopod is a top-down affair.

I use a sturdy but light Bogen/Manfrotto monopod, topped by an armless tilt head. The tilt head rocks vertically, if need be, and I just twist my body to sweep horizontally. You may need (from a camera store) a tiny adapter ring to match the quarter-inch bolt that sticks up atop the monopod to a three-eighths-inch hole in the bottom of some tilt heads (despite their being made by the same maker). Why this discrepancy? Beats me: *caveat emptor*. Some Bogen/Manfrotto monopods have legs with three sections, some with only two. Get the one with three; it closes more compactly, an advantage for traveling, and you can adjust it more easily for sitting.

When using binoculars, I put a T-bar on the tightened tilt head. (Or you can remove that tilt head altogether.) The crosspiece of the T is a six-inch length of one-inch PVC pipe. I drilled holes all the way through the pipe (in one side, out the other), pushed a quarter-inch bolt through the holes, and threaded that bolt to one end of a connector nut, which is the leg of the T. The other end of the connector nut attaches to the bolt on the tilt head (or the one atop the monopod). I rest my binocs *across* the crosspiece, not along its length. This way, I can roll them vertically as if they were lying across a cylindrical railing (which they are).

Using a monopod takes a little practice, but soon it becomes second nature. I now use one as an optics support far more than I expected to when I first tried it. For me it has become a key birding tool. When I work a habitat very slowly, a monopod lets me search continuously, arms relaxed, as long as my interest holds—with this exception: when it comes to ptarmigans, my search's limit now depends not so much on my interest as on my faith in them, which, after those dawn vigils at eleven thousand feet, approaches my faith in unicorns.

CAMOUFLAGE

Birders sometimes want to look less conspicuous to birds, especially when stalking. Anecdotes abound about how bright (or, worse, white) clothing startles many birds—especially, it often seems, those birds one most ardently seeks. Legendary birds like quetzals and becards and trogons are famously wary of brightly garbed birders. What to do? First, wear muted colors. Sometimes, though, these seem to soothe people but not birds. This is probably because even earth-toned clothes, if washed in detergents that have brighteners, will reflect some of sunlight's ultraviolet wavelengths. To us they have a fresher look; to birds, many of which can see into ultraviolet wavelengths, that shirt may well glow alarmingly.

At the other extreme from electric blue or red, camouflage—or "camo"—beckons. Hunters know it works. We birders could learn a lot from hunters if we cared to or dared to, because we hunt, too, even if without guns. Of course, birders who wear camo open themselves to other birders' teasing and to the astonished looks of passers-by; so try just a slipover camouflage T-shirt, to don or doff as the occasion suggests. By moving to the side of the trail and blending quietly into dappled underbrush, even sitting there awhile, those with thick enough skin to wear camo may get the last laugh with the closest looks at shy birds.

Camouflage breaks up contours and outlines, letting the wearer blend into leafy habitats. But using camo to best effect requires common sense. A birder defeats it by looming as a silhouette against the sun, or by rising fast from the under-brush, or by making jerky movements with binoculars, or by suddenly pointing, or by whipping out a noncamo hand-kerchief, or by not standing still. And a group of camo-wearing birders on the beach would look like invad-ing Marines, a scenario that should cause even the toughest of us to blush.

Camouflage has some potentially fatal drawbacks. In deer season a camouflaged birder may end up as a trophy. And in some violent places where birdwatching is a tourist pastime but likely to be misunderstood by the locals—say, in Colombia—a camouflaged birder may be caught in a crossfire that has nothing to do with the game warden.

Birds reward the concealed observer.

Short of camo, even the timid among us can wear a hat with a wide brim—one of those intrepid, safari-style hats—or a cap with a bill, such as a baseball cap. On sunny days the brim or bill casts a shadow over one's eyes and so makes them less prominent. On all days it breaks up the full face. In "Stalking," I shared Byron Butler's suggestion of how to turn this slight help into almost an art form. I repeat the matter here because it is such an easy way to gain a small advantage. Besides shading the eyes, wearing a hat reminds a birder of how powerful an image a face is, and circumspection naturally follows. Maybe this is why some hats seem to be lucky ones.

In wide-open places—sometimes even in the forest—a more common, but more elaborate, ruse upon birds comes into play with blinds (the "hides" of the British). And elaborate is right, if not in the United States, where a certain rusticity is *de rigeur*, then in Britain, where hides may be palatial. The birder who has the patience to stay put and use a blind, even one that is little more than an upended box or a dull sheet draped over a branch, will find that birds, after their initial alarm at such a strange structure, reward the concealed observer by going about their business in ways that roving birders scarcely ever see.

MIRRORS AS POINTERS

Pointing—so natural an act, so hard a habit to break—often scares away nearby birds. Anchoring the elbow to the waist lowers and shortens the pointing arm and so makes it much less alarming. (Yes, alarming: when was the last time someone pointed at you?) But it also makes it harder to sight along. A friend tells me that in the remote mountains of Papua New Guinea people point with the chin, and in the American Southwest so do (or once did) the Navajos—a gentler gesture still, but even harder for the rest of us, unaccustomed to such subtlety, to follow.

Pointing— a hard habit to break.

Using words to point out a little bird in a big tree can defeat the best of us: "There, on that limb twenty feet up that goes to the right. No, the next one, the thinner one. Now go out six feet. See where part of it sort of, uh, bends down? No, I mean bends away and ... There it goes." Turning a tree or a scene into a clock and putting the bird on its hour—a tactic mentioned earlier—helps to focus eyes on an area, but it does not really pinpoint a spot.

Worse, confronting a whole hillside of trees and shrubs, how does anyone point out a skulking bird? Naming some distinctive plant may work for some; the rest of us are botanical ignoramuses, so it simply adds to the confusion. In Texas recently some friends, trying to help me get on a Gray Vireo, kept whispering, "In that cactus! In that cactus!" Well . . . hmm . . . which cactus? Plants are something all birders annually resolve to learn to recognize, along with getting more exercise and living better.

When the sun shines, I use a cosmetics mirror to point out birds in foliage. First, I waggle its reflection on the ground close by to get control of it. Then my companion can follow the patch of light as I brush it toward that tree, twenty feet up the trunk and out six feet along that thin limb to the right. I don't shine it directly on the bird, because a sudden blast of light from below may startle it away. But I encircle the target or say, "a yard to the right of the light now," and that works.

A mirror can bounce a little patch of sunlight surprisingly far and over a much wider arc than just more or less back toward the sun. Clouds or haze pose a problem, but then we are no worse off than before we took up this trick. Laser pointers ought to work, too, but their bright but extremely narrow beams disappear in daylight's full brightness. Even so, the best of them do make a visible mark in deep forests and on very gray days or at twilight.

THE BOOKMOBILE

As beginners, my friends and I delved into our field guides after the briefest glance at a bird. We looked like a roving book group. The object of our interest flitted before us unobserved while we pored over pictures of it. As a result, our impression of the dynamic bird was often stifled by its static, printed image. Nature beckoned; books won.

As we became better birders, we opened our field guides less often. We seized instead the chance at hand to watch the bird itself. We left our books in the car, to consult if need be while memory was fresh. For the most part, this habit has stuck; I attend to the bird without the distraction of a book. But on a recent trip far from home, I found myself opening a fellow birder's field guide disconcertingly often in the field. Some old ways die hard.

Nowadays I keep my field guides in two sturdy cartons in my car's trunk, along with tapes and CDs of bird sounds, manuals about various bird families, maps and where-to-bird books, assorted tree and flower and butterfly and dragonfly guides, even a dictionary of bird names. Into those cartons, too, go sections of books I have extracted from their covers and rebound into picture-filled brochures. (Some friends, shocked at my surgery, call these books butchered; I think of them as tailored.) That trunk is a library; that car, a bookmobile. Another box in there holds seed for sparrows, trail mix for me, hand lenses and spotting scope eyepieces, tools, index cards for taking notes, a tide table, and lucky hats. A rough frame of 2 x 4s braces the boxes to the side. Scope, tripod, monopod, tape recorder, camera, and other pricey gear take over the center of the trunk when I go birding. I take them with me when I am done birding; the books and hats can stay there.

A further word about those butchered books. Mostly they are books about bird families. I use their slim extracts more than I do complete volumes. These are the pages that sort out *Empidonax* flycatchers and *Calidris* sandpipers, fall warblers and winter sparrows, and gulls all year long—bird families that call for all the pocketed guidance I can muster when I need it, not back at home or even back in the car with the rest of the library. They are like mentors in my vest.

Most days the bookmobile's books go unread, but they are there to leap into action as arbiters of disputes, authorities on plumage and range, and resources in a pinch, even as lunchtime reading. In the field, I can focus entirely on a perplexing bird, confident that, back at the car, I can turn to far more information than I hold in my head or even in my

Loading the bookmobile.

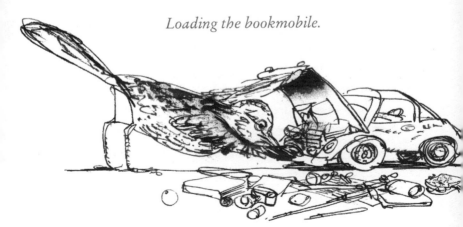

vest. Sometimes this bookmobile system misfires; my pocketed pages do not bear on the strange bird I have heard or glimpsed, and I have failed to notice what my bulkier authorities, waiting back there at the car, tell me I should have looked at hardest. That sends me back to recheck the bird—if it is still there—and teaches me to look, next time, more thoroughly than ever before. And if this happens often enough, it persuades me that for some group rife with perplexities or rich with rarities I had better get out my knife and tape and make still another pamphlet, another vest-pocket expert.

Far from home and from my bookmobile, I usually do carry an intact field guide with me. Far from home, my identifications get tentative, my miscalls odd and alarming—a beginner's angst all over again. Then I cherish my field guide as a life vest. I try not to use it, but I pat it from time to time for reassurance.

LEADING BETTER
CLUB TRIPS

FIFTEEN STEPS

For many years I avoided leading club trips or even going on many of them. The little outings of little clubs once seemed to me so . . . elementary, even dull. Eventually I got off this high horse, and I wish I had done so long before. Most club trips, even slow-paced ones, can provide plenty of good birding. And droll? If only more days were droll! Leading club trips hones birding skills. Now I not only lead them, I also go along on as many as I can that others lead. This supports those leaders and they in turn teach me all sorts of lessons about how to lead better trips—as well as all sorts of lessons about birds.

In this chapter I have tried to summarize a great many suggestions about how to make club trips click. The result is an awful lot of advice, so much that, to help the reader, I have been lavish in using **bold print** to stress what I think are **key matters**. I have organized the advice into fifteen steps, but I will go through them in just ten parts, because some of them go together so naturally. Here are my fifteen steps:

1. Rehearse the trip in the field.
2. Start on time.
3. Ask and remember what people want from the day.
4. Briefly explain your theme, goal, and itinerary.
5. Carpool—and make the fewest possible stops.
6. Review a few rules at the first birding stop.
7. Ask and field questions, and honor them all.
8. Pay most attention to the beginners.
9. Plan ahead for the people you wish had stayed home.
10. When you ID birds, briefly explain.
11. When you are wrong or stumped, say so and explain why.
12. Make sure everyone sees or hears the good birds.
13. Don't feel guilty about the birds that don't turn up.
14. Know when to wind down, size up, and stop.
15. Draft your trip report before you go to bed.

If you hesitate to lead a club trip, two ways to ease into the role are to **lead some half-day trips yourself and co-lead other, full-day ones.** The brevity of the former challenge and the companionship of the latter should allay fears. True enough, toward the end of some long trips with lots of participants of widely ranging experience and expertise, I have found myself working hard and blundering in the effort. Once, drained or deranged, I thought a California Towhee

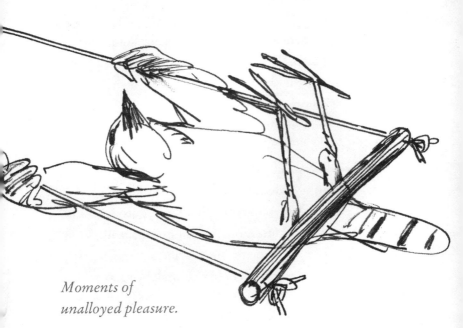

Moments of
unalloyed pleasure.

on a nearby corral fence was a Golden Eagle on a distant ridge. A companion deflected my crazy announcement. But even the most frazzling club trips redeem themselves with shared moments of beauty and pleasure and fun (what the trip, after all, is for). And, invariably, by showing birds to others, one sees those birds afresh oneself. The leader always learns the most.

Having fun is the main goal of a club trip. As a leader, I seek good birds for the day. But I try, as well, to provide each participant, and especially each beginner in the group, with some moments of unalloyed birding pleasure. These may be "Audubon Moments" that we all share. Or they may be those little thrills when the bird itself clearly answers a good question. Or they may be keen identifications independently achieved. More than any tally, these particularly intense encounters with nature, it seems to me, are what make days afield memorable, and so I try my best to make them happen.

STEP 1: REHEARSING THE TRIP

Rehearse the trip beforehand, and in the field. Why bother to prepare so thoroughly? Because other birders have put their day in your hands. Sometimes a club trip travels so far afield that a test run is out of the question except for leaders who do nothing but go birding. But most club trips are fairly local. A dry run a few days or (at most) a week ahead is not only feasible, it's a pleasant excuse for another outing with birding companions.

Here are some of the **avian angles** to test and refine on such an occasion:

PREDICTABLE BIRDS. Now is when you discover that all the wintering ducks have left the lake. Or the shorebird migration is already in full swing. Or some irruptive species has appeared unannounced or disappeared despite all the hoopla. These surprises will help shape your itinerary. Of course, some of the best birding is unpredictable even a week ahead—for example, warbler waves.

MOLTS. Are there gulls or terns or ducks in interesting plumages and states of feather wear that suggest themselves as points of focus during the upcoming trip?

NESTS. Casual birders see the nests of very few species. In spring and summer, take time to search for them during a

Proud parents and their outrageously cute babies.

rehearsal. A couple of pieces of dull string discreetly tied to some twigs will mark the spots, like clues on a treasure map. Caution: Both in rehearsal and on the trip day itself, approach nests with great care. Jays and other nest robbers all too often follow the heedless birder. But a nest with a brooding parent or, even better, with outrageously cute babies—even if viewed only for a moment, glanced at in passing without breaking stride, or spied on from afar—can make a birder's day.

SPRING OR SUMMER SINGERS THAT APPARENTLY ARE ON TERRITORY. Now is the time to stake them, so you can count on them a week later.

And here are some of the **logistical matters** I look into:

WHAT ROADS OR BIRDING TRAILS ARE UNEXPECT-EDLY CLOSED, or what else might affect access? Are there **difficult places** on the trail that could stymie someone who turns up for the trip? Do places charge **entrance fees**? (At the start of the trip, ask who has passes.) If you are beside the sea, what will the **tides** be like on trip day? Tides really move birds around. Does your trip coincide with some hunting or fishing season? Shooting days, especially, can be hellish for birding; fly fishermen, on the other hand, often stand wonderfully still.

WHAT IS THE MILEAGE AND DRIVING TIME FROM STOP TO STOP? Look carefully at **parking** at each stop: how many parking places, how easy to manage as cars converge and birders organize their gear. These situations will affect how insistently I carpool, and they may even affect my choice of places to stop at all.

*A difficult place
on the trail.*

*Not everyone
is absorbed
beyond
hunger.*

WHAT IS THE WALKING TIME AT EACH PLACE? Figure a slow pace. On even a leisurely club trip, you are birding against the clock. The dawn chorus, shorebirds' movements with the tides, birds' siesta time, afternoon coastal winds and mountain storms, weekend crowds materializing in birdy places like parks, a rural festival and its traffic on your route, daily commerce coming alive along the riverfront or the harbor—considerations like these affect when and how long you can spend at each place, and they affect the order in which you visit them.

WHERE IS A GOOD PLACE TO HAVE A PICNIC? Lunch can be early, but (I have learned) it should not be late. Not everyone will be absorbed beyond hunger. And lunch breaks have a way of breaking a trip's momentum, so I try to schedule them between a substantial change of habitats or after one that is likely to be especially exciting. That way, the lunch break is like an intermission between acts.

WHERE ARE THE TOILETS ALONG THE WAY? A cavalier attitude toward excretion can upset the bashful. Work these facilities into the schedule so they do not all appear at the day's last stop. In fact, one should turn up, heaven-sent, along about the second stop.

From this rehearsal, you can gain several crucial **trip-planning aids.**

A REALISTIC ITINERARY. Club trips are not speed contests or marathons. I find a club trip can comfortably explore

*Find a good place
for a picnic.*

Where are the toilets?

only about two-thirds of the stops I have birded during a rehearsal. I save the others as alternatives if we encounter No Fly Zones (see page 27) or as add-ons if the day has moved along swiftly and I feel the requisite energy still in the group (that is, not just in me). Knowing about them and yet skipping them is the cost of doing business and the sign of a canny leader.

A LIST OF SPECIFIC BIRDS AND SIGHTS. These may be high points (a reliable rarity) or they may be comic relief (those cute babies), but for a leader they are welcome moments to count on.

A THEME FOR THE TRIP. Will you focus on a big list? On identifying female ducks or other particularly difficult birds? On comparing the suites of birds in two or three habitats? On some technique like birding by ear or ID'ing hawks aloft? As they do for musicians, rehearsals give trip leaders familiarity, insight, and interpretational ideas. A rehearsal is when a club trip's strategy emerges; the trip itself allows only tactics.

A SENSE OF WHAT TO AVOID TRYING TO DO. The dry run lets you know what birds do not seem to be there at all, what routes are just not going to work, what places are too time-consuming or in some other way not worth the effort this time around. Save them for next time, even if that makes your heart ache. Edit your plans.

Now you know what material you have to work with. **Make yourself an actual paper map and itinerary, or at least a timetable,** no matter how loosely you expect to stick to it or how well you know the route. **Fill in a mock anticipatory checklist.** This list will remind you of where to seek particular species. It will also flag species or whole groups of them that you want to be especially prepared for. You may want to do some homework! You may even want to be sure to bring along one of your homemade brochures—for warblers or sparrows, for example. The hour it takes to make these on-paper preparations will ease your mind before the trip. And on the trip itself, when things are bound to happen that confound your expectations, you will be able to exploit the nice surprises and accommodate the nasty ones, and do both with rehearsed ease.

One nasty surprise on a trip can be a twisted ankle, a bad cut, or some other minor injury. As part of any rehearsal I check my car's first aid box. The car will be closer than a drug store. It may seem crass, but in this litigious age, on arduous trips I now also have everyone in my group sign a waiver that frees the club from liability for mishaps, trivial or horrendous. Dig up a copy on rehearsal day. Calamities like car crashes, heart attacks, strokes, or other mayhem are like rocks that can fall from the sky but, in my experience, hardly ever do. Even so, a few discreet souls in any crowd should know how to deal with more than the usual scrapes and bruises—and not just on birding trips. Spending a few Saturday mornings in a Red Cross class is all it takes to learn some coping methods. But hardly anyone does. Birders or not, old or young (but especially old), we can all benefit from knowing more than the clumsiest first aid, even as we hope never to have to use it.

STEPS 2, 3, 4: GETTING THE TRIP UNDERWAY

Start on time. Birding is most often a morning pursuit. Most club trips get into the field after dawn. In many habitats birds have already had their most active hours of the day, so you are already playing catch-up. Yet you cannot rush the group from the start—or at all. I sometimes announce club trips as "fast-paced, varsity" ones, but of course they all end up the same way, as leisurely reunions with the delightful excuse of birding. All the more reason, then, to start on time.

I arrive at our meeting place early and make noticeable pre-departure noises and moves. There are always preliminaries, late arrivals, and lingering chores. Unavoidably, carpooling means last-moment delays, too. The challenge is to **shepherd without barking**. I cajole and encourage my birders to do what they really do want to do anyway, which is to go birding.

Social note: If there are strangers present, I introduce myself quickly as we convene, and with something more than "Hi! My name is Todd, and I'll be your leader today." Some leaders have everyone say names, but most people on club trips already know each other. If they don't, this hurried ritual will scarcely help when strangers convene or when a few newcomers meet the regulars. Instead, I urge everyone to introduce themselves to whomever they seem to fall in with during the day. On a trip with lots of club members, newcomers are bound to be shy, so they need encouragement if they are ever to speak. Part of my job is to make them do that over the hours, but not at the very start, when their awkwardness is bound to be at its worst. By a good day's end, they will feel at ease.

Shepherd without barking.

I poll the whole group quickly—just a show of hands—about **experience and skill levels**: varsity, intermediate, beginner. This lets me know right away who should get my particular attention during the day (always the beginners) and who can help me most (the varsity). And this poll lets beginners affirm their greenness frankly instead of whispering it apologetically in the course of things. I have never found this candor to offend, and it seems to give novices at least the courage of confession. This is when I urge the better birders to look around and plan to help the beginners. And I tell the beginners that **they will "learn" only three birds today, but that neither they nor I know which birds or when.** They must not overwhelm themselves with the day's many other species, which they will meet again. (As the day goes on, I will ask the beginners which birds may have made their select lists, and why.)

Next I ask **what people especially want to get out of the day**. It is *their* trip, after all; I am *their* leader. Birders on trips may have goals—species, skills, experiences—that depart widely from what their leaders assume. A few moments sharing hopes and goals let us all become one another's guides.

Now I turn to what I hope to make **the trip's theme and goals**. These are the plans I hatched during that rehearsal last week. A few sentences suffice. After all, I have the whole day to develop my plans. But some well-edited words help at the start: "This morning let's concentrate on birding by ear." "This is Father's Day, so let's find proud bird daddies and their babies." "I'd like to devote an hour to sorting through gulls." "Let's go for a hundred species today." "The Rare Bird Alert reports species X at the gulch; let's try to find it when we are there." (But I try not to plan around rarities unless they are thoroughly staked. Club trips are not occasions for vigils.)

Finally, the **itinerary**. It is always short. Not all club trips involve driving, but many do, even if we are going to spend all day in one place. A trip with more than a few stops decays toward roadway entropy. How long will the trip last? Are there any handicaps in the group (like my own gimpy leg) that we should take into account? Who has to leave early? Let's quickly arrange those early rides back now. I mention all the stops, and then I mention the first one again as **where we'll all meet next**. Sometimes that first stop is where other birders plan to join us. On this score, it is a real kindness to late risers and people coming from a distance to announce in advance, in any printed publicity, where the group expects to be birding at, say, eight o'clock (and then to be there).

Now I negotiate carpools. Next, can we leave our cars here, where we are organizing ourselves, or is there a good place on the edge of town? Finally, **does everyone have all their gear—even their binoculars?** Lunch? Anyone need to pee even before we start? Cars have gas? Uh-oh, a slight delay there: go get gas and we'll meet you at the first stop.

"Does everyone have all their gear?"

STEP 5: CARS

Driving is not birding. It gets us where we want to go, but it gets in the way, especially for the folks in the back of the van or, worse, the back of a caravan. Birding, not driving, should rule the day. Some trips cannot avoid being slow motorcades in which everyone scours the skies and fields along the way and leaps in and out of the cars from time to time. But on most trips, we bird place by place. The fewer places, the less driving. The less driving, the more birding and so the better the trip.

Rule: The more cars on the trip, the fewer the feasible stops. Corollary: Carpool even if only for part of the time. William Beebe said, "In jungle work one person is a necessity, two are a crowd." The same holds for cars. In one car, we scarcely notice where we park or the sudden movement we make when birding while driving. But with many, each stop is like stabling horses. The closer to one the number of cars, the better. Four really is the practical limit for birding. For one thing, four stopped cars need a real parking lot, not just a wide shoulder. And four cars can slam sixteen doors. Lately, locking some cars makes them flash their lights and honk—just the thing to scare off nearby robbers and birds. And four cars starting up can sound like race time at Le Mans. Even if there are only two, and especially if there are more, the driver of the final car should know at all times where the caravan is going.

A caravan is not a car rally. Keep speeds modest on the highway even if you plan to meet next at a place everyone knows. Do not dash through yellow traffic lights. By sticking together, the caravan can respond as one to the albatross that flies over the highway. (An albatross did fly over New Jersey's Garden State Parkway recently, although not during a club trip.) But if that big bird overhead is not an albatross and your caravan is more than two cars long, **try not to stop alongside the road.** A roadside stop may be great for the first car or two, but it mostly mystifies the birders farther back. I have been in lines so long that we in the rear have watched Lark Sparrows that birders in the front cars never saw when they stopped for Vesper Sparrows that we never saw. And roadside stops risk accidents: if you stop at a birdy place on a quiet country road, almost certainly an eighteen-wheeler will careen past you.

It may sound techie, but FRS two-way "family" radios make fine caravanning tools. They unite the fragmented group when someone shouts "Caracara!" or they ease the perplexity of birders behind when birders ahead halt. Of course, birders have gotten along perfectly well for generations without them, but why pass up a way to communicate en route at last? Cell phones do not work away from their towers, and that is where birders often go. Rely instead on FRS two-way radios. (The ABA urges birders to use Channel 11, so we are all on the same band.) Be sure to read the helpful counsel in *Pete Dunne on Bird Watching* for more on these nifty gadgets. Keep cell phones for emergencies (and hope they work).

One emergency everyone can avoid is keys locked in cars. The shrewd driver always carries an **extra car key** in a deep pocket or duct-tapes one to the back of a license plate or the inside of a hubcap, even if only for the day. My extra key has graced the back of a license plate for ten years, and I have used it twice. It's so simple!

STEPS 6, 7: DON'TS AND DO'S

I wait until the trip's first real stop to go over things like rules and customs. This way, latecomers are there to hear them, too. Most of the group has had a chance to settle in by then. If we start birding right where we initially meet, I often walk awhile before pausing to go over don'ts and do's, lest I pile on too much at the very start of a trip. No one wants a lecture at a time like this. But I have found that a few commonsense rules are especially worth mentioning briskly. I don't delay this matter much, lest what I intend to be ordinary suggestions seem to be prompted by someone's gaffe already that very day. And of course many club trippers are old hands who don't need this sort of instruction at all, and you can skip it. Here is a rather long list from which I choose just a few items according to the feel of the day.

First, the don'ts:

DO NOT SLAM CAR DOORS. Birds will hear us approaching like an artillery barrage or the hunters in *Peter and the Wolf.*

AVOID LOUD TALKING. It alarms birds, deafens birders, and adds to the noise from which we may be trying to isolate signals (see "Listening" page 107).

DON'T GET AHEAD OF THE LEADER. People should not move into the terrain we are about to bird. They will flush birds or send them under cover, and so we will never even know what we missed. They create rambling No Fly Zones.

DON'T STARE AT THE LEADER. On the rim of the stupendous Black Canyon of the Gunnison, I once watched a dozen visitors as they listened to a ranger. As he talked, a Golden Eagle swept close by them at eye level, then soared out grandly over the abyss. Not an eye turned from the ranger. We are taught that it is impolite to look away when listening. But looking away is precisely what a birding trip is about: it is about looking at *birds.* When, as leader, you are talking, make your group keep its eyes on the habitat.

DO NOT WANDER OFF WITHOUT TELLING THE LEADER. Wanderers may wander into where we are headed, even by going off to the side. And they distract a leader who is having a busy enough day finding birds, without having to find birders. Some souls crave solitude, but a club trip may not be the best occasion for that. To stick together is not to march along in school trip formation, but a group of birders should not have to be rounded up. The leader is not a cowboy.

Birders lingering behind the main group are no problem. But if the habitat is confusing, occasional announcements of where we are going will help hapless stragglers. Once, while on a woodland bird walk, I went into a privy and emerged to find the leader and everyone else had disappeared. Paths diverged over steep, forested slopes that blocked all views. Baffled, I could only go back to the trailhead and steam for two hours until the group returned, of course with tales of great birds. "Where were you?" they all asked.

And some do's:

WHOEVER CANNOT SEE THE BIRD OR EVEN FIGURE OUT WHAT BIRD WE ARE LOOKING AT SHOULD SAY SO FRANKLY. The major leaguer Jon Dunn has pointed out to me how easy it is to tell who has and hasn't seen the bird, just from their facial expression and tone of voice. When we are on a bird, that is not the time for self-abnegation: "Oh, yes, I think I saw it." That is courtesy backfiring. We are *all* there to see birds. (On the other hand, I have heard mad tales of couples coming to actual blows over who was hogging the scope.)

Focus on the bird, not the book.

FOCUS ON THE BIRD, NOT THE BIRD BOOK. Each of us brings eyes and ears to the encounter. Share the bird; pocket the book. Don't read, *look*.

WHEN POINTING, KEEP YOUR ELBOW ON YOUR WAIST. Pointing is a very hard habit to break, because it feels so natural and is so helpful. But sudden or intrusive movements alarm wild creatures. With a little practice, one can point slowly and discreetly, elbow on the waist, perhaps with all fingers together so it looks more like a blessing than an arrow.

ASK QUESTIONS. A trip without questions is a trip without shape. As a leader, I try now and then to help club

Point discreetly.

trippers **frame questions that the birds and habitats can answer in the field.** Questions of this sort do not come easily (see "Asking Questions in the Field" page 75); many lack focus, definition, acuity; they are like blurry vision. Other questions seek answers that depend on ambitious interpretations rather than modest observations. Shyness, too, can make questions flounder. Contrary to widespread denial, there are stupid questions, plenty of them. But that is no reason not to ask them. Perhaps just by looking at the bird together we can answer them. At least we can refine them. I think the pleasure of finally getting one's question right, and of nature itself answering, can be a highlight of a day afield.

EVERY GOOD QUESTION DESERVES AN ANSWER. But no leader has the answer to every one. Does anyone else know that question's answer or how to puzzle it out? I take notes (real ones, on paper) and try hard to find postponed answers and get back to the inquirers (even if they have forgotten they asked). This follow-up may seem excessive, but asking good questions is a core goal of my bird club trips. A good question that you cannot answer merits a search, not a shrug.

WHOEVER HAS TO LEAVE EARLY SHOULD TELL THE LEADER (AGAIN) AT THAT TIME. Otherwise, at day's end the leader's nightmare looms: "Where's Harry?"

It can be hard to remember what to look at and listen to.

STEP 8: HELPING BEGINNERS

Beginning birders, even enthusiastic ones, often do not feel very comfortable as a club trip gets underway; and the more birds encountered, the more a beginner may feel at a loss. Novices are daunted not only by birds but also by more experienced birders. Discreetly and nicely, skilled birders on club trips should help the beginners. What they are now, we were then.

Think back to when you began birding. Often you could not find the bird at all—a voice in the foliage, a speck in the sky. Just as often you could not imagine what trait to look at or listen to. Think what novices confront: "It sings like a creeper." Huh? a what? "Purple Finches have a cleaner vent." A cleaner what? "Check that hummingbird's rectrices," "that

Experienced birders should help the beginners.

duck's speculum," "that sparrow's malar," "that gull's gonys." When the bird in front of you is compared to one you have never seen or described by traits you have never heard of, that is a prescription for confusion and discouragement. Anticipate these little disasters; help beginners through them.

As a leader, **I try to make sure each beginner identifies three species without anyone's help.** I may hover like a parent quail, but these sorties are the beginners' own shaky steps to competence and confidence, and so these are among the most important moments of their day. Interrogations by the birds themselves ("All right, who am I?") focus a lot of the trip's rambling commentary. The beginner's interrogations in response ("All right, then, what are your traits?") are signal moments. Cultivate them, and you will make the day memorable for that new birder.

I also have beginners practice raising and aiming binoculars. First we go through the motions (see page 89) on big birds like sitting ducks. Then we try our new skill on tinier targets. Surprisingly often, more birders than just beginners

Have beginners practice aiming their binoculars at sitting ducks.

will say, "This is the first time I have ever gotten my binoculars right on a sparrow." No wonder sparrows confuse!

Some years ago on BirdChat, Gail Mackiernan suggested another vital service that club trip leaders can render beginners, especially ones who are having trouble locating birds in their binoculars. Sometime during the day, she wrote, we can check their binoculars. Are they in alignment? Does the novice understand what the individual eye-adjustment gizmo is for and how to set it? (For starters, just set it at zero.) Are the lenses clean? (Bring a cleaner.) Offering this help is not being too technical; it is aiding someone in real distress.

STEP 9: BAD AND NOT SO BAD TRIPPERS

Some birders do complicate club trips. One is the **self-appointed expert** (SAE), second-guessing your IDs or announcing birds when you have asked everyone to puzzle them out quietly. Maybe by asking, "Hmm, what do you think?" now and then, you can let the know-it-alls share the limelight they seem to crave. If they really are good birders, so much the better; it adds that many more sharp eyes and ears. If they aren't so good, I try to make sure my corrections are circumspect, lest I appear to have hung anyone out to dry—or lest anyone feel that way, since vanity and vulnerability so often go together. Everyone else can see what is going on, so **there is never a need to score points.** Some leaders try to get SAEs to help shepherd the group; I prefer not to. Others did not come on this trip for that. In the long run, the soundest way to deal with SAEs, I think, is to make an effort toward real acquaintance and hope that first impres-

The self-appointed expert.

sions were misleading. But what if, to your chagrin, first impressions were right—and then they show up again next time? At least you know they like your trips!

More perplexing are the **perfectly nice birders who cannot stop talking**. Some keep comparing today's birds enthusiastically with better birds on better trips. Others seem to have everything but birding on their minds. Politely shush them, yes, but how . . . the fourth time? I have found myself stretched trying to accommodate them, but I have to get on with the trip as best I can. And so, resigned to it, I try to keep them nearer to my ear than to others'. If they keep talking loudly, I keep whispering to them; sometimes they catch on.

Another odd sort of tripper is what some inspired commentator has called "**room service**." These birders order up a species and wait for delivery. Some of them have traveled widely and have huge life lists, yet they seem unable to identify species themselves or even to see much that hasn't been pointed out to them. Sometimes they scarcely look at what is pointed out. Why have they come along? I treat them kindly, but as birders of dim ornithological promise.

The ardent but infirm: I have been lame myself, both when I started birding long ago and again recently. As the leader, you know your day's itinerary, and so you can adjust it, within limits, for people who cannot handle the whole thing. Go over the route you have planned and let them reckon their chances of managing it. If they say they can't, you might select especially birdy parts of it that are accessible to them and suggest they focus their efforts there while you take the rest of the group on. Then have them report what they have seen and heard in your absence. Very likely they will have a lot to report. After all, the patient observer who lets a few habitats open themselves at their own pace—recall "Standing Still" and "Camouflage"—will reap rewards easily equal to those that come from charging about the landscape. But steering an ardent birder off a tough route can be poor advice. Recently a leader urged me to skip a steep climb in Newfoundland. I complied, had a birdless day—and missed, of course, still another ptarmigan.

Kids. They are their parents' charge, not yours. Some kids are splendid birders, so don't brush them off! If you do, they will remember you when they are major leaguers or, worse, when they aren't birders at all anymore and think about why and decide it's all your fault. But if they are boisterous (not surprisingly), some candid words to their parents may be in order: "Can you go that way while we go this way, and let's meet at ten o'clock?" But beware, lest you rush in where diplomats fear to tread.

Finally, I must mention a legendary figure among trip leaders. After particularly fine birds, he smiles, nods slightly, and declares quietly, "Very nice. . . . Next?" His voice echoes Noel Coward's. His timing rivals Jack Benny's. Bewitched, I have found myself adopting his signature remark. I have come to think of it as the ultimate club trip compliment.

Chatterers.

*Sometimes, as I explain aloud how
I identified the bird, I realize with dismay . . .*

STEPS 10, 11: EXPLAINING ID'S

Club birding trips are basically bird-identification trips. If, as leader, I want my birders to keep their noses out of books, I must tell them, while they look at the bird, what they would find in a book about its identifying traits. Calling out (but not too loudly) the clues and criteria can be lively: "Yow! Get a load of that gray cheek!" or "Look! You can actually see the slightly webbed toes!" When the occasion is not so thrilling, I set the ID against that of a similar species; if we have found a moorhen, I may ask why it isn't just a colorful coot, or why that young Song Sparrow isn't a Lincoln's Sparrow, or why that grosbeak's song isn't a robin's song or why a Downy Woodpecker isn't a Hairy. Since I have made my way to my own ID, it is just a matter of doing it again out loud.

Explaining ID's aloud has an added benefit for me: it forces me to focus on that very bird. It makes me look or listen freshly. As I tick off traits, I confront them anew, renew my grasp of them; and sometimes, alarmed, I find myself uncertain. Which woodpecker has those spots on the outer tail feathers? Oh yes, Downy! Which dowitcher has greater wing covert feathers with buffy edges? Hmm. Here is the bird itself to tell me again, even as I tell others.

While no good ID of a species rests on a single trait, most rely on rather few. So it is not time-consuming to go through them for the group or to quiz others about what they are. "What about just the bill tells us that bird is a Hutton's Vireo, not a Ruby-crowned Kinglet?" "How do its wings tell us that female Gadwall isn't a female Mallard?" "Which accipiter is that, and by what three clues?" In the course of these reviews, we may recognize details we have forgotten we even look at. Take time to dwell on them. **I often ask people, once they have identified a bird, to stay on it, watch it, for a slow count of five.** It always startles me how much one can see in those few seconds, and how one can do it over and over again with the same species and still see an unfamiliar mark.

In fact, this is a good habit anytime, and especially if glance-and-go is creeping in, when the temptation is to whisk one's binocs away from the bird at the very moment of acquaintance. As a rule of thumb, take a little too long over each bird.

Sometimes while enumerating traits aloud, I realize with dismay that my ID is wrong. Traits I am rattling off become traits that don't match the bird after all. The bird has caught me out. All intermediate and even varsity birders who lead trips have this unenviable experience from time to time, especially those of us who tend to get people on a bird by calling out our first impression even as we continue to look or listen. It is humbling, but not humiliating. So I cancel my call and start again, chastened. What, then, can that bird be? **Work it out, and out loud.** Everyone is interested now; the leader is sweating! Here is real excitement! Worse, if it is far away, is it even a bird? I recall the Barn Owl that turned into a tree stump, the Black-crowned Night-Heron that, when someone asked, "Is it near that half-buried white-walled tire?" became the tire. Character-building time.

STEPS 12, 13:
WHEN THINGS GO RIGHT OR WRONG

Club trips thrive on common birds, but rare ones do turn up. Rarity makes for attraction, but I have already counseled against featuring rarities on club trips unless they are tethered for the occasion. Uncommonly fine views are superb occasions, too. So are baby birds; who on earth can look at them and not smile? And behavioral moments that are ordinary enough to the birds may be extraordinary to us:

Black-crowned Night-Heron turning into a half-buried tire.

moments of chase and escape, of courtship and conquest, even of sleep. **Make sure everyone shares the trip's special encounters.** They are occasions to pause for and sights to delight in and to share. Even twitchers secretly rejoice in them.

But sometimes the gods refuse to produce some bird you want. There is no muse of birdwatching to appeal to, nor does your lucky hat work. Today the bird will not show itself. It may be the hundredth species for the day, or the local specialty a visitor has tagged along to find, or the rarity you really did risk counting on. **Give your goal your best try; but if you fall short, yield gracefully.** When Churchill said, "In victory magnanimity, in defeat defiance," he was not talking about birding. Even if people have paid for the trip—and some clubs do charge nonmembers—no one, not even a "room service" type, has paid for the very bird you cannot find. One of the nice things about club trips is that they are not pricey tours. You are volunteering your role in this trip, and so, come to think of it, are the birds. If you must apologize for perfidious Nature, apologize with a wink.

STEP 14: AS THE TRIP WINDS DOWN

The early hours' euphoria has passed; you have reached the third or fourth place on the itinerary; the day begins to wear on. Sometimes even by lunchtime, I try to **be alert for signs of flagging stamina**. Some participants may have left for home by now. Conversation is replacing focus. These people are not yet tournament tough. This is when I trim my plans. A club trip should end with most participants still feeling pretty energetic. Sometimes I call an early halt to the

Be alert for signs of flagging stamina.

official day and say I am going to continue informally myself and anyone is welcome to come along. Even then, I tend to postpone further real exertion until another day. What is to be gained by plunging on, except fatigue? On a club trip I try to keep plans in proportion and tailor them as the day wanes. I try to **know when to stop.** I will lead these birders again; they should not tremble at the prospect.

A little before we go our separate ways, when I do not expect another high point, I **ask the participants to say what were for them the high points of the day.** I do not mean, "How did I do, Coach?" Rather, a trip's winding down is the occasion to share then and there what are already recollections. For some they are of special birds like lifers and RIEs (see page 33); for others they turn on widely acknowledged or perhaps quite personal "Audubon Moments." The variety of impressions often surprises me, as it does the people sharing them. By now most people in the group have met most others. Much more than social introductions at the day's start, this common pause at its end seems to bring the group together in companionship.

STEP 15: THE REPORT

Even as I lead a club trip, I anticipate writing the report of it for the club newsletter. This way, I see the day with a reporter's eye; and as soon as I get home, I work up my story. **I write up a draft by bedtime and let it sit overnight.** If I let the report go longer before starting, it grows stale. If I file it right away, I risk purple passages. Perusal the next day reveals them. I fix them and file.

Remember that the club newsletter's trip report is really for the participants who came along. They will read it the way people who were at a ball game like to read about it in the newspaper the next day—for that warm feeling, "I was there." Their own recollections will fill in the part of the story you forgot to tell. Meanwhile, birders who were not along are not likely to pore over your piece.

Report, don't rhapsodize. Focus on a memorable event during the trip or on a few especially remarkable finds, and add a species count. Far fewer than two hundred words ought to do it, unless you have an extraordinary tale to tell.

There, the story is in. You are done!

Write a draft of the trip report by bedtime.

BIBLIOGRAPHY

American Ornithologists' Union. 1998. *Check-List of North American Birds*, 7th ed. Washington, D.C.: American Ornithologists' Union.

Arbib, Robert. 1972. On the art of estimating numbers. *American Birds* 26 (September): 706-12.

Attenborough, David. 1998. *The Life of Birds*, in ten episodes. London: BBC Video.

Beebe, William. 1958. The high world of the rain forest. *National Geographic Magazine* 113 (June): 838-55.

Bent, Arthur C. 1919-68. *Life Histories of North American Birds*, vols. 1-26. Washington, D.C.: U. S. National Museum.

Birders Journal. 1998. *The Basics of Bird Identification: Bird Topography*. Whitby, Ontario, Canada: Birders Journal Publishing, Inc.

Butler, Byron. 1996. What color should I wear while birding? *The Horned Lark* (newsletter of the Kansas Ornithological Society) 23 (March): 7-8. (Online in 2005 at www.ksbirds.org/kos/Color.htm.)

Chauvin, Rémy. 1967. *The World of an Insect*. London: Weidenfeld and Nicolson.

Connor, Jack. 1988. *The Complete Birder*. Boston: Houghton Mifflin.

Cooke, Charles. 1941. *Playing the Piano for Pleasure*. New York: Simon & Schuster.

Dewey, John. 1934. *Art as Experience*. New York: Minton, Balch, and Company.

Dittmann, Donna, and Greg Lasley. 1992. How to document rare birds. *Birding* 24 (March): 145-59. (Online in 2005 at www.northbirding.com/raredoc/document.html.)

Dunne, Pete. 2003. *Pete Dunne on Bird Watching*. Boston: Houghton Mifflin.

Elkins, James. 1996. *The Object Stares Back*. New York: Simon & Schuster.

Gombrich, Ernst. 1960. *Art and Illusion*. Princeton: Princeton University Press.

Grant, Peter, and Killian Mullarney. 1989. *The New Approach to Identification*. Hunstanton, England: Witley Press.

Hall, Edward T. 1959. *The Silent Language*. Garden City: Doubleday.

Hall, Edward T. 1966. *The Hidden Dimension*. Garden City: Doubleday.

Hartshorne, Charles. 1973. *Born to Sing: An Interpretation and World Survey of Bird Song*. Bloomington: Indiana University Press

Heinrich, Bernd. 1989. *Ravens in Winter*. New York: Simon & Schuster.

Hutchinson, Evelyn. 1965. *The Ecological Theater and the Evolutionary Play*. New Haven, Conn.: Yale University Press.

James, William. [1902] 1999. *The Varieties of Religious Experience*. New York: Random House.

Jardine, Ernie. 1996. *Bird Song Identification Made Easy*. Toronto, Ontario, Canada: Natural Heritage / Natural History, Inc.

Jellis, Rosemary. 1977. *Bird Sounds and Their Meaning*. Ithaca, N.Y.: Cornell University Press.

Kieran, John. 1947. *Footnotes on Nature*. Garden City: Doubleday.

Kroodsma, Donald. 2005. The Singing Life of Birds. Boston: Houghton Mifflin Company.

Lack, David. 1956. *Swifts in a Tower*. London: Chapman and Hall.

Lofting, Hugh. [1920] 1948. *The Story of Doctor Dolittle*. Philadelphia: Lippincott.

Lorenz, Konrad. 1952. *King Solomon's Ring*. New York: Crowell.

MacKay, Barry K. 2001. *Bird Sounds*. Mechanicsburg, Pa.: Stackpole Books.

Orenstein, Ronald. 1997. *Songbirds*. San Francisco: Sierra Club Books.

Patterson, Mike. 2004. How to write convincing details. (Online in 2005 at www.pacifier.com/~mpatters/details/details.html.)

Pettingill, Olin S., Jr. 1951. *A Guide to Bird Finding East of the Mississippi*. New York: Oxford University Press.

Pettingill, Olin S., Jr. 1953. *A Guide to Bird Finding West of the Mississippi*. New York: Oxford University Press.

Poole, Alan, Stettenheim, Peter and Gill, Frank eds. 1992–2002. *The Birds of North America*, vols. 1-18. Philadelphia: The Birds of North America, Inc. (American Ornithologists' Union and Academy of Natural Sciences of Philadelphia).

Pope, Alexander. [1711] 1944. *Essay on Criticism*. New York: Dover.

Powers, Alan. 2003. *BirdTalk*. Berkeley: Frog, Ltd.

Rothenberg, David. 2005. *Why Birds Sing*. New York: Basic Books.

Sibley, David. 2002. *David Sibley's Birding Basics*. New York: Knopf.

Skutch, Alexander. 1996. *The Minds of Birds*. College Station: Texas A&M University Press.

Slinger, Joey. 1996. *Down and Dirty Birding*. New York: Simon & Schuster.

Stap, Don. 2005. *Birdsong*. New York: Scribner.

Stevens, Peter. 1974. *Patterns in Nature*. Boston: Little, Brown and Company.

Stilgoe, John R. 1998. *Outside Lies Magic*. New York: Walker Publishing.

Tinbergen, Niko. 1961. *The Herring Gull's World*. New York: Basic Books.

Walton, Richard, and Robert Lawson. 1999. *Birding by Ear: Western North America*. Boston: Houghton Mifflin. Compact disks.

Walton, Richard, and Robert Lawson. 2002. Rev. ed. *Birding by Ear: Eastern and Central North America*. Boston: Houghton Mifflin. Compact disks.

Walton, Richard, and Robert Lawson. 2002. Rev. ed. *More Birding by Ear: Eastern and Central North America*. Boston: Houghton Mifflin. Compact disks.

White, Milton. 1961. *Listen, the Red-Eyed Vireo*. Garden City: Doubleday.

Young, Jon. 1996. *Learning the Language of Birds*. Audio cassette tapes. Duvall, WA: Owlink Media.

The writer, TODD NEWBERRY, was assured in college that watching birds was too much fun for a respectable career. He turned instead to another fascination, deciphering the rules that govern the growth and form of modular animals (that is, clonal ones, such as most corals and, his particular pets, sea squirts). He joined the University of California, Santa Cruz, at its heady beginning and, as an emeritus professor, still teaches there—and, at last, about birds.

The artist, GENE HOLTAN, was born on the Canadian prairies, which, dry as they were, had enormous populations of water birds. After many years in Santa Cruz, he now lives in Oakland, California, with what appear to be the same birds. He has devoted a long life to the visual arts, painting and drawing in media ranging from paper to canvas to pottery to children's books. Now, as Todd chases birds, Gene goes to his studio, where large abstract paintings have him in their grip.